Yours truly, I. HERMANN

Memoirs of a Veteran

Who served as a Private in the 60's
in the War between the States

Personal Incidents, Experiences and Observations

Written by
CAPT. I. HERMANN
Who Served in the Three Branches of the Confederate Army

Cherokee Publishing Company
Atlanta, Georgia

Library of Congress Cataloging in Publication Data

Hermann, I. (Isaac), 1838-1917.
  Memoirs of a confederate veteran, 1861-1865.

  Reprint. Originally published: Memoirs of a veteran,
Lakemont, Ga. : CSA Press, c1974.
  1. Hermann, I. (Isaac), 1838-1917. 2. United States--
History--Civil War, 1861-1865--Personal narratives,
Confederate. 3. Confederate States of America. Army.
Georgia Infantry. Regiment, 1st (1861-1862)--Biography.
4. Confederate States of America. Army. Georgia
Artillery. Martin's Battery--Biography. 5. Confederate
States of America. Army. Georgia Artillery. Howell's
Battery--Biography. 6. Georgia--History--Civil War.
1861-1865--Personal narratives. 7. Soldiers--Georgia--
Biography. I. Title.
E605.H55 1984   973.7'458   84-17655
ISBN 0-87797-068-8

This book is printed on acid-free paper which conforms to the American National Standard Z39.48-1984 *Permanence of Paper for Printed Library Materials*. Paper that conforms to this standard's requirements for pH, alkaline reserve and freedom from groundwood is anticipated to last several hundred years without significant deterioration under normal library use and storage conditions.

Manufactured in the United States of America

Originally published in 1911
Jacket by Orran L. Hudson

ISBN: 978-0-87797-068-2 Hardcover
ISBN: 978-0-87797-319-5 Paper

Cherokee Publishing Company
P O Box 1730, Marietta, GA 30061

INTRODUCTION.

The following reminiscences after due and careful consideration, are dedicated to the young, who are pausing at the portals of manhood, as well as womanhood, and who are confronted with illusory visions and representations, the goal of which is but seldom attained, even by the fewest fortunates, and then only by unforeseen circumstances and haphazards, not illustrated in the mapped out program for future welfare, greatness and success.

Often the most sanguine persons have such optimistic illusions, which, unless most carefully considered will lead them into irreparable errors. Even the political changes, often times necessary in the government of men, are great factors to smash into fragments the best and most illusory plans, and cast into the shadow, for a time being at least, the kindliest, philanthropic and best intentions of individual efforts, until the Wheel of Fortune again turns in his direction, casting a few sparks of hope in his ultimate favor, and which is seldom realized.

If the reader of the above has been induced to think and carefully consider, before acting hastily, the writer feels that he has accomplished some good in the current affairs of human events.

CHAPTER I.

A PICTURE.

Entering the post-office for my daily mail, I noticed in the lobby, hanging on the wall, a beautiful, attractive and highly colored landscape and manhood therein displayed in its perfection, gaudily dressed in spotless uniforms; some on horse-back, some afoot, with a carriage as erect and healthful demeanor that the artist could undoubtedly produce; he was at his best, setting forth a life of ease and comfort that would appeal to the youngster, patriot and careless individual, that therein is a life worth living for. Even the social features have not been omitted where men and officers stand in good comradeship. Peace and repose, and a full dinner pail are the environment of the whole representation.

It is the advertisement of an army recruiting officer, who wants to enlist young, healthy men for the service of the executive branch of our National Government, to defend the boundaries of our territory, to protect our people against the invasion of a foreign foe, to even invade a foreign land, to kill and be killed at the behest of the powers that be, for an insult whether imaginary or real, that probably could have been settled through better entente, or if the political atmosphere would have thought to leave the matter of misunderstanding or misconstruction to a tribunal of arbitration.

The writer himself was once a soldier; the uniform he wore did not correspond with that of the picture above, it was rather the reverse in all its features. He enlisted in the Confederate service in 1861, when our homes were invaded, in defense of our firesides, and the Confederate States of America, who at that time, were an organized Government.

Usually an artist, when he represents a subject on canvas, uses a dark background, to bring forth in bright relief, the subject of his work. But I, not being an artist, reverse the matter in controversy, and put the bright side first.

OTHER PICTURES.

When in 1861 the Southern States, known as the Slave States, severed their connection with the Federal Government and formed a Confederacy of their own, which under the Federal

Constitution and Common Compact, they had a perfect right to do, they sent Commissioners, composed of John Forsyth, Martin J. Crawford and A. B. Boman to Washington, with power to adjust in a peaceable manner, any differences existing between the Confederate Government and their late associates. Our Government refrained from committing any overt act, or assault, and proposed strictly to act on the defensive, until that Government, in a most treacherous manner, attempted to maintain by force of arms, property, then in their possession and belonging to the Confederate Government, and which they had promised to surrender or abandon. But on the contrary, they sent a fleet loaded with provisions, men and munitions of war, to hold and keep Fort Sumter, in the harbor of South Carolina, contrary to our expectations, and as a menace to our new born Nation.

Then, as now, there were State troops, or military organizations, and being on the alert, under the direction of our Government, and under the immediate command of General Beauregard, they fired on the assaulting fleet to prevent a most flagrant outrage, and after a fierce conflict, the Fort was surrendered, by one Capt. Anderson, then in command.

Abraham Lincoln, the then President of the United States, called out 75,000 troops, which was construed by us as coercion on the part of the Federal Government, so as to prevent the Confederates from carrying out peaceably the maintenance of a Government already formed. To meet such contingency President Jefferson Davis called for volunteers. More men presented themselves properly organized into Companies, than we had arms to furnish. Patriotism ran high, and people took up arms as by one common impulse, and formed themselves into regiments and brigades.

The Federal Government, with few exceptions, had all the arsenals in their possession. We were therefore not in a condition to physically withstand a very severe onslaught, but when the Northern Army attempted on July 21, 1861, to have a holiday in Richmond, the Capital of the Confederate States, we taught them a lesson at Manassas, and inscribed a page in history for future generations to contemplate.

So Mounting a Stump, I Proceeded to Introduce Myself.

CHAPTER II.

The Federal army under General Scott consisted of over 60,000 men, while that of General J. E. Johnston was only half that number. Someone asked General Scott, why he, the hero of Mexico, had failed to enter Richmond. He answered, because the boys that led him into Mexico are the very ones that kept him out of Richmond.

The proclamation of Abraham Lincoln calling out for troops was responded to with alacrity. In the meantime, we on the Confederate side, were not asleep; Washington County had then only one military organization of infantry called the Washington Rifles, commanded by Captain Seaborn Jones, a very gallant old gentleman, who was brave and patriotic. The following was a list of the Company's membership, who, by a unanimous vote, offered their services to the newly formed Government to repel the invader: (See Appendix A.). Their services were accepted, and they were ordered to Macon, Ga., as a camp of instructions, and for the formation of a regiment, of which the following companies formed the contingent—their names, letters, and captains. (See Appendix B.)

J. N. Ramsey, of Columbus, Ga., was elected Colonel. We were ordered to Pensacola, Fla., for duty, and to guard that port, and to keep from landing any troops by our enemy who were in possession of the fort, guarding the entrance of that harbor. This was in the month of April, 1861. From Pensacola the regiment was ordered to Northwestern Virginia. The Confederate Capital was also changed from Montgomery, Ala., where the Confederate Government was organized, and Jefferson Davis nominated its President, to Richmond, Va.

About the middle of May, the same year, twenty-one young men of this County, of which the writer formed a contingent part, resolved to join the Washington Rifles, who had just preceded us on their way to Virginia. We rendezvoused at Davisboro, a station on the Central of Georgia Railway. We were all in high spirit on the day of our departure. The people of the neighborhood assembled to wish us Godspeed and a safe return. It was a lovely day and patriotism ran high. We promised a satisfactory result as soldiers of the Confederate States of America.

At Richmond, Va., we were met by President Davis, who came to shake hands with the "boys in gray", and speak words of encouragement. From Richmond we traveled by rail to Staunton, where we were furnished with accoutrements by Colonel Mikel Harmon, and which consisted of muskets converted into percussion cap, weapons, from old revolutionary flint and steel guns, possessing a kicking power that would put "Old Maude" to shame. My little squad had resolved to stick to one another through all emergencies, to aid and assist each other and to protect one another. Those resolutions were carried out to the letter as long as we continued together. We still went by rail to Buffalo Gap, when we had to foot it over the mountains to McDowell, a little village in the Valley of the Blue Ridge. Foot-sore and weary we struck camp. The inhabitants were hospitable and kind, and we informed ourselves about everything in that country, Laurel Hill being our destination.

An old fellow whose name is Sanders, a very talkative gentlemen, told us how, he by himself ran a dozen Yankees; every one of us became interested as to how he did it, so he stated that one morning he went to salt his sheep in the pasture—all of a sudden there appeared a dozen or more Yankee soldiers, so he picked up his gun, and ran first, and they ran after him, but did not catch him. We all felt pretty well sold out and had a big laugh, for the gentleman demonstrated his tale in a very dramatic way.

The following morning, we concluded to hire teams to continue our journey, which was within two days march of our destination. We passed Monterey, another village at the foot of the Alleghany Mountains, about twelve miles from McDowell. We crossed the Allaghany into Green Brier County, passed Huttensville, another little village at the foot of Cheat Mountain, from there to Beverly, a village about twelve miles from Laurel Hill, where we were entertained with a spread, the people having heard of our approach. We camped there that night, and passed commandery resolution upon its citizens, and their kind hospitality. The following day we arrived at Laurel Hill, where the army, about 3,000 strong, was encamped. The boys were glad to see us, and asked thousands of questions about their home-folks, all of which was answered as far as possible. The writer being a Frenchman, a rather scarce article in those days in this country, elicited no lit-

tle curiosity among the members of the First
Georgia Regiment. Sitting in my tent, reading
and writing, at the same time enjoying my pipe,
I noted at close intervals shadows excluding the
light of day—looking for the cause, the party or
parties instantly withdrew. Major U. M. Irwin
entered; I asked him the cause for such curiosity, he stated laughing, "Well, I told some fellows we'd brought a live Frenchman with us.
I suppose those fellows want to get a peep at
you." I at once got up, mounted an old stump,
and introduced myself to the crowd: "Gentlemen, it seems that I am eliciting a great deal of
curiosity; now all of you will know me as Isaac
Hermann, a native Frenchman, who came to
assist you to fight the Yankees." Having thus
made myself known, I took the privilege to ask
those with whom I came in contact their names,
and what Company they belonged to, and thus
in a short time I knew every man in the Regiment. We were now installed and regularly
enrolled for duty.

CHAPTER III.

Laurel Hill is a plateau situated to the right of Rich Mountain, the pass of which was occupied by Governor Wise, with a small force.

In the early part of July, General McClelland, in command of the Federal troops, made a demonstration on our front. Our position was somewhat fortified by breastworks; the enemy came in close proximity to our camp and kept us on the Qui-vive; their guns were of long range, while ours would not carry over fifty yards. Picket duties were performed by whole companies, taking possession of the surrounding commanding hills. Many shots hissed in close proximity, without our being able to locate the direction from which they came, and without our even being able to hear the report of the guns. Very little damage, however, was done, except by some stray ball, now and then. It was the writer's time to stand guard, not far in front of the camp, his beat was alongside the ditches. In front of me the enemy had planted a cannon. The shots came at regular intervals in direct line with my beat, but the shots fell somewhat short, by about fifty to seventy-five yards. I saw many hit the ground.

When Lieutenant Colonel Clark, came round on a tour of inspection, I remarked, "Colonel, am I placed here as a target to be shot at by those fellows yonder. One of their shots came rather close for comfort." He said, "Take your beat in the ditch, and when you see the smoke, tuck your head below the breastworks"—which was three and one-half feet deep the dirt drawn towards the front, which protected me up to my shoulders. For nearly two hours, until relieved, I kept close watch for the smoke of their gun, which I approximated was about a mile distant, and there I learned that it took the report of the cannon eight seconds to reach me after seeing the smoke, and the whiz of the missel four seconds later still; this gave me about twelve seconds to dodge the ball—anyhow, I was very willing when relief came, for the other fellow to take my place. In the afternoon, minnie balls rather multipherous, were hissing among the boys in camp, but up to that time there was no damage done, when a cavalryman came in and reported that some of the enemy was occupying an old log house situated about a half mile in front of us, and it was there through the cracks of that building came the missiles that made the fellows dodge about. General Garnett, our Commander, ordered out

two companies of infantry, who, taking a long
detour through the woods placed themselves in
position to receive them as they emerged from
the building, and with two pieces of artillery,
sent balls and shells through their improvised
fort. Out came the "Yanks" only to fall into
the hands of those ready to give them a warm
reception.

On that evening, three days rations were
issued. At dark it commenced drizzling rain;
we were ordered to strike camp, and we took up
the line of march to the rear, when I learned
that the enemy had whipped out Governor
Wise's forces on Rich Mountain and threatened
our rear. We marched the whole of that night,
only to find our retreat to Beverly blockaded
by the enemy who had felled many trees across
the road, the only turn-pike leading to that
place.

We had to retrace our steps for several miles,
and take what is known as mountain trail, leading
in a different direction, marching all day.
The night again, which was dark and dreary
multiplied our misgivings. The path we followed,
was as stated, a narrow mountain path,
on the left insurmountable mountains, while on
the right very deep precipices; many teams that

left the rut on account of the darkness, were precipitated down the precipices and abandoned. Thus, after two nights and one day of steady marching, we arrived at Carricks' Ford, a fordable place on the north fork of the Potomac River. The water was breast-deep, and we went into it like ducks, when of a sudden, the Yankees appeared, firing into our column. They struck us about and along the wagon train, capturing the same, while the advance column stampeded. We lost our regimental colors, which were in the baggage wagon, in charge of G. W. Kelly, who abandoned it with all the Company's effects, to save himself.

Colonel Ramsey, in fact all our officers were elected on account of their cleverness at home. This being a strictly agricultural country, the men and officers knew more about farming than about military tactics. Colonel Ramsey was an eminent lawyer of Columbus, Georgia. He gave the command, "Georgian, retreat," and the rout was complete. It was a great mistake that the Government did not assign military men to take charge in active campaigns; many blunders might have been evaded and many lives spared at the beginning of the war.

One half of my regiment was assigned as rear

guards and marched therefore, in the rear of the column behind the wagon train. We were consequently left to take care of ourselves the best we could. General Garnett was killed in the melee. Had we had officers who understood anything about military tactics. these reminiscences might be told differently.

As soon as we heard firing in our front, we at once formed ourselves into line of battle, in a small corn patch across the stream, on our immediate right, at the foot of a high mountain. It seemed to have been new ground and the corn was luxuriantly thick. The logs that were there were rolled into line, thus serving as terraces, and also afforded us splendid breastworks. We were hardly in position, when artillery troops appeared and crossed the ford, not seventy-five yards from where we were in line, seeing them, without being seen ourselves. Major Harvey Thompson, who was in Command of our forces, which were not over four hundred and fifty strong, seeing some men making ready to fire, gave orders not to fire, as they were our own men crossing the stream, and thus lost the opportunity of making himself famous, for it proved to be the enemy's artillery in our immediate front. Had he given orders to fire and charge, we could have been on them before they could possibly have formed themselves into battery, captured their guns, killed and captured many of their men, and would have turned into victory what proved to have become a disastrous defeat.

Thus being cut off from our main forces, who were in full retreat, and fearing to be captured, we climbed the mountain in our rear, expecting to cut across in a certain direction, and rejoin our forces some distance beyond. Thus began a dreary march of three days and four nights in a perfect wilderness, soaked to the bone and nothing to eat, cutting our way through the heavy growth of laurel bushes, we had to take it in Indian file, in single column.

Many pathetic instances came to my observation; some reading testaments, others taking from their breast-pocket, next to their heart, pictures of loved ones, dropping tears of despair, as they mournfully returned them to their receptacle. An instance which impressed itself forcibly on my mind, was the filial affection displayed between father and son, and in which the writer put to good use, the Biblical story of King Solomon, where two women claimed the same child, but in this instance neither wanted to claim. It was thus: Captain Jones found a piece of tallow candle about one inch long in his haversack, and presented it to his son, Weaver, saying, "Eat that, son, it will sustain life;" "No, father, you eat it, I am younger than you, and stronger, and therefore can hold out longer." There they stood looking affectionately at each other, the Captain holding the piece of candle between his fingers. So I said, "Captain, hand it to me, I will divide it for you." Having my knife in hand, I cut it lengthwise, following the wick, giving each half, and passing the blade between my lips. It was the first taste of anything the writer had had in four days.

CHAPTER IV.

When night overtook us, we had to remain in our track until daylight would enable us to proceed. When at about nine o'clock A. M. word was passed up the line, from mouth to mouth—"A Guide! A man and his son who will guide us out of here." Then Major Thompson, who was in front sent word down the line for the men to come up. The guides sent word up the line to meet them half way, that they were very tired, so it was arranged that Major Thompson met them about center, where the writer was. The guides introduced themselves as Messrs. Parson, father and son. The senior was a man of about fifty years, rather ungainly as to looks, and somewhat cross-eyed, while his son was a strong athletic young man, about twenty-three. They said they were trappers, collecting furs for the market. It must be remarked that that country was perfectly wild, and uninhabited, for during all this long march I had not seen a single settlement, but it contained many wild beasts, such as bears, panthers, foxes, deer, etc. He related that a tall young man by the name of Jasper Stubbs, belonging to Company E, First Regiment, Washington Rifles, came to his quarters very early this morning, inquiring if any soldiers had passed by, saying he found a nook under a projecting rock where he stood in column the night before, and to protect himself from dew, he lay down to rest, and fell asleep. When he awoke, it was day and he found his comrades gone, and that he was by himself. The surface of ground or rock, was a solid moss-bed, consequently he could not tell which way our tracks pointed, and he happened to take the reverse course which we went, and thus came to where the Parsons lived. Stubbs was missing, thus proving that the men's story must be true. It must also be remembered that the majority of the people in Western Virginia were in sympathy with the enemy, and thus possessed of many informers or spies, who would give information as to our whereabouts and doings.

A conference was held among the officers as to what was best to be done. Parson claimed to be in sympathy with the South, and he knew that we would not be able to carry out our design, and that we would all perish, so he put out to lead us out of our dilemma. Major Thompson was for putting the Parsons under arrest, and force them to lead us in the direction we first assumed, or perish with us. Parsons spoke up and said, "Gentlemen, I am in your power; the country through which you propose to travel is not habitable, I have been raised in these regions, and there is not a living soul within forty miles in the direction you propose to go, and at the rate you are compelled to advance, you would all perish to death, and your carcasses left for food to the wild beasts of the forest." The conference was divided, some hesitated, others were for adopting Major Thompson's plan, when the writer stepped forward, saying, "Gentlemen, up to now, I have obeyed orders, but I for one, prefer to be shot by an enemy's bullet, than to perish like a coward in this wild region." Captain Jones tapped me on the shoulder, remarking; "Well spoken, Hermann, those are my sentiments—Company E, About Face!". Captain Crump, commanding Company I, from Augusta, Ga., followed suit, and thus the whole column faced about, ready to follow the Parsons.

The writer made the following proposition: That Mr. Parson and son be disarmed, for both carried hunting rifles; that I would follow them within twenty paces, while the column should follow within two hundred yards, thus in case of treachery they would be warned by report of my gun, that there is danger ahead. These precautions I deemed necessary in case of an ambush. Addressing myself to our guides, I said, "Gentlemen, you occupy an enviable position; if you prove true, of which I have no doubt myself, you'd be amply rewarded, but should you prove otherwise, your hide is mine, and there is not enough guns in Yankeedom to prevent me from shooting you." At this point, a private from the Gate City Guards, whose name is Wm. Leatherwood, remarked, "You shall not go alone, I will accompany you." I thanked him kindly, saying I would be glad if he would. Thus we retraced our steps, following our leaders, when after about three miles march we struck a mountain stream, in the bed of which we waded for nine miles, the water varying from knee to waist deep, running very rapidly over mossy, slippery rocks, and through gorges as if the mountains were cut in twain and hewn down. In some places, the walls were so high, affording a narrow dark passage, I don't believe God's sun ever shone down there. I was so chilled, I felt myself freezing to death in mid summer, for it was about the 17th of July; darkness was setting in, and I had not seen the sun that day, although the sky was cloudless, when to my great relief we came to a little opening on our left, the mountain receding, leaving about an acre of level ground, with a luxuriant growth of grass. Our guides said they lived within a quarter of a mile from there. I said, let us rest and wait for the rest of the men. When after a little rest, I started again, I was too weak to make the advance, although provisions were in sight. I had to be relieved, and some others took my place, while I lay exhausted on the grass. Happily some of the men had paper that escaped humidity; loading a musket with wadding, they fired into a rotten stump, setting it on fire, and by persistent blowing, produced a bright little flame, which soon developed into a large camp fire, around which the boys dried themselves.

Parson proved himself a noble, patriotic host. After a couple of hours, he sent us a large pone of corn-bread, baked in an old-fashioned oven. I received about an inch square as my share,—the sweetest morsel that ever passed my lips. It was sufficient to allay the gnawing of my empty stomach,—it had a strange effect on me, for every time I would stand up, my knees would give way and down I went otherwise I felt no inconvenience.

It was a remarkable fact that every man was able to keep up with our small column and we did not lose a single man up to that time.

CHAPTER V.

The next morning Mr. Parson drove up two nice, seal fat beeves,—to get rations was a quick performance, and the meat was devoured before it had time to get any of the animal heat out of it, some ate it raw, others stuck it on the ramrod of their gun and held it over the fire, in the meantime biting off great mouthfulls while the balance was broiling on his improvised cooking utensil. Mr. Parson also brought us some meal, which being made into dough was baked in the ashes, and thus we all had a square meal and some left to carry in our haversack.

Mr. Parson was tolerably well to do, he owned some land, raised his truck, had a small apple orchard, and indulged in stock-raising. He owned several horses and some of the officers bought of him. The writer feeling badly jaded, also concluded he would buy himself a horse, and paid his price, $95.00 for a horse, but Major Thompson, being of a timid nature, was afraid that too many horsemen might attract attention, refused to let me ride by the wagon-road, so Mr. Parson said there was a mountain path that I could follow that would lead in the big road some few miles beyond, but that I would have to lead the animal for about a couple of miles, when I would be able to ride. Dr. Whitaker, a worthy member of my Company, and a good companion, offered me his services to get the animal over the roughest part of the route. I accepted his offer, and promised that we would ride by turns, so I took the horse by the bridle and led him, Whitaker following behind, coaxing him along. The mountain was so steep I had to talk to keep the horse on his feet, but nevertheless he slipped several times and we worried to get him up again. We made slow headway; the column had advanced, and we lost sight of it, and were left alone, worrying with the horse, who finally lost foothold again, and rolled over. The writer was forced to turn loose the bridle to keep from being dragged along into the hollow. The horse rolled over and over, making every effort to gain his feet, but to no avail, until he reached the bottom, where he appeared no bigger than a goat. I felt sorry for the poor animal, so I went down, took off his saddle and bridle, placed them on a rock, and left him to take care of himself. I rejoined Dr. Whitaker. Relieved of our burden, we followed the trail made by the column. About sunset we caught sight of them, just as they crossed Green Brier River, a wide, but shallow stream. At that place the water was waist deep in the center, running very swift, as mountain streams do, over slippery moss-covered rocks. When center of the river, I lost foot hold and the stream, swift as it was, swept me under, and in my feeble condition I had a struggle to recover myself. I lost my rations, which were swept down stream, a great loss to me, but undoubtedly served as a fine repast for the fishes which abounded in those waters.

The column continued its line of march, passing a settlement, the first dwelling I had seen in five days. I called at the gate; receiving no answer, I walked into the porch; the door being ajar, I pushed it open and found an empty room, with the exception of a wooden bench, and an old-fashioned, home-made primitive empty bedstead, with cords serving to support the bedding that the owners had hurriedly removed before our arrival. I called again. Presently a young woman presented herself. After passing greetings of the day I asked, "Where are the folks?" She said, "They are not here," (the surroundings indicated a hasty exit). I said, "So I see. Where are they?" She said she did not know, undoubtedly not willing to divulge. "Who lives here?" "Mr. Snider." "And you don't know where he is?" "No, he heard you all were coming, and not being in sympathy with you all, he left." "Well, he ought not to have done so, nobody would have harmed him or hurt a hair on his head. He is entitled to his opinion, as long as he does not take up arms against us." So I recounted the accident that had befallen me, and wanted to replenish my provisions. I asked if I could buy something to eat. She said, "There are no provisions in the house", "Well, I hope you would not object to my making a fire in this fire-place to dry myself." She said she had no objection. It must be remembered that the fire-places in those days were very roomy indeed. I found wood on the woodpile, and soon had a roaring fire. It was late in the evening, and I intended to pass that night under shelter, for I was chilled to the bone. In moving the bench in front of the fire, on which to spread my jacket to dry, I noticed a pail covered, and full of fresh milk, "Well, you can sell me some of that milk, can't you?" She said, "You can have all you want for nothing." I thanked her and said I wish I had some meal and I could well make out. She said, "I will see if I can find any", and presently she returned with sufficient to make myself a large hoe-cake. I baked the same on an old shovel. While it was baking my clothes were drying on my body, affording a luxuriant steam bath. I had a tin cup. I drank some of the milk and had a plentiful repast. I handed her a quarter of a dollar to pay for the meal, which she accepted with some hesitancy. All at once the girl disappeared and left me in charge. It was most dark, when someone hollowed at the gate; recognizing the voices, I found them to be two men of my Company, viz., G. A. Tarbutton and J. A. Roberson. I met them and invited them in. To tell the truth, I did not much like the mysterious surroundings of those premises, especially as the girl asked me not to divulge that she let me have some meal.

My comrades and self took in the situation; we conferred with one another and agreed to spend the night under shelter in a warm room, a luxury not enjoyed in some time and not to be abandoned. They had informed me that the Column had encamped less than a quarter of a mile beyond and they had returned to this place in search of some Apple Jack. We concluded to take it by turns, while two of us are asleep, the third will stand guard and keep up the fire, for the reader must know that notwithstanding the season, the nights were very cold in those mountain regions and were especially so with wet garments on.

The following morning my comrades left, but before leaving we disposed of the milk in the pail. I remained in the hope of again seeing my charming hostess, and induce her to sell me some provisions for my journey along. I saw in the woods, some old hens scratching, and I thought I might persuade her to sell me one. Presently she came with a plate of ham, chicken and biscuits which she offered me. I accepted, and not wishing to embarrass her, did not ask any questions. Presently, old man Snider appeared. He was a fine looking specimen of manhood, had a ruddy complexion and appeared physically Herculean. After exchanging a little commonplace talk, he followed me to where the boys camped. He was seemingly astonished to see so many gentlemen among the so-called savage rebels. I asked him if he could induce his daughter to bake me a chicken, he answered, "I suppose I could." "What will it be worth?" "Half a dollar" he guessed. I gave him the money and he said he would bring me the chicken, which he did, and it was a fine one, well cooked.

The people in that thinly populated section of the country lived a very primitive life, they were mostly ignorant. They did their own work, had plenty to live on, owned no negroes and were very kind-hearted after you got acquainted. They had strange notions about the Rebels, thinking we were terrible fellows. The original settlers of Northwestern Virginia were Dutch, a very simple and hard-working honest people.

At about three o'clock in the afternoon, having had a long rest, we again took up the line of march by short stages, still under the guidance of one of our guides, and from that day on, we continued our march, passing Cheat Mountain, Allegheny Mountains, until finally we reached McDowell. Coming down Cheat Mountain, the boys were treated to a strange sight, especially those who were raised in a low country and who had never seen any mountains, for in those days there was not much traveling done, and the majority of the people did not often venture away from their homes.

The little village of Huttensville lies just at the foot of Cheat Mountain, a mountain of great altitude. The houses below us did not appear to be larger than bird cages, but plainly in view, first to the right and then to the left, as the pike would tack, the mountain being very steep. It was a lovely day, the sun had risen in all its splendor, when as if by magic, our view below us was obscured by what seemed to be a very heavy fog, and we lost sight of the little village. Still the sun was shining warm, and as we were going down hill it was easy going, and as we approached the village, the veil that had obscured our view lifted itself and the people reported to have experienced one of the heaviest storms in their lives, the proof of which we noticed in the mud and washouts which were visible, while we who were above the clouds did not receive a single drop.

CHAPTER VI.

At McDowell we formed a reunion with the rest of our forces, who in their flight made a long detour, passing through a portion of Maryland adjoining that part of West Virginia. The following evening we had dress parade and the Adjutant's report of those who were missing. The writer does not remember the entire casualties of that affair, but found that his little squad of twenty-one were all present or accounted for.

My friend, Eagle, from whom we hired teams to carry us to Laurel Hill was present and he came to shake hands with me while we were in line; he was glad to see me. A general order to disband the regiment for ten days was read, in order to enable the men to seek the needed rest. Mr. Eagle came to me at once, saying, "I take care of you and your friends, the twenty-one that I hauled to Laurel Hill, at my house. It shall not cost you a cent", a most generous and acceptable offer. I called for my Davisboro fellows, and followed Mr. Eagle to his home, where he entertained us in a most substantial manner. He was a man well-to-do, an old bachelor. The household consisted of himself and two spinster sisters, all between forty and fifty years of age; and a worthy mother in the seventies, also a brother who was a harmless lune, roving at will and coming home when he pleased, a very inoffensive creature; his name was Chris. The mother, although for years in that country, still could not talk the English language. Untiringly and seemingly in the best of mood, they performed their duties in preparing meals for that hungry army. Chris got kinder mystified to see so many strangers in the house. He walked about the premises all day, saying, "Whoo-p-e-ee Soldiers fighting against the war", and no matter what you asked him, his reply was, "Whoo-o-p-e-ee, Soldiers fighting against the war-ha-ha-ha-ha!"

At the expiration of the ten days leave, we bade our host good-bye. We wanted to remunerate him, at least in part, for all of his trouble in our behalf, but he would not receive the least remuneration, saying, "I am sorry I could not have done more." We rendezvoused in the town, but a great many were missing on account of sickness, the measles of a very virulent nature having broken out among the men, and many succumbed from the disease. We were ordered back to Monterey and went into camp. The measles still continued to be prevalent and two of my Davisboro comrades died of it, viz., John Lewis and Noah Turner, two as clever boys as ever were born. I felt very sad over the occurrence. Their bodies were sent home and they were buried at New Hope Church.

General R. E. Lee, rode up one day, and we were ordered in line for inspection, he was riding a dapple gray horse. He looked every inch a soldier. His countenance had a very paternal and kind expression. He was clean shaven, with the exception of a heavy iron gray mustache. He complimented us for our soldiery bearing. He told Captain Jones that he never saw a finer set of men. We camped at Monterey for a month. During all this time, when the people at home became aware of our disaster, they at once went to work to make up uniforms and other kinds of wearing apparels. Every woman that could ply a needle exerted herself, and before we left Monterey for Green Brier, Major Newman, who always a useful and patriotic citizen, made his appearance among the boys, with the product of the patriotic women of Washington County. Every man was remembered munificently, and it is due to the good women of the county that we were all comfortably shod and clothed to meet the rigorous climate of a winter season in that wild region.

CHAPTER VII.

While still in camps at Monterey, the Fourteenth Georgia Regiment, on their way to Huntersville, with a Company of our County, under command of Captain Bob Harmon, encamped close to us. The boys were glad to meet and intermingled like brothers. A day or so after we were ordered to move to Green Brier at the foot of the Allegheny and Cheat Mountains, the enemy occupying the latter, under general Reynolds.

Our picket lines extended some three miles beyond our encampment, while the enemy's also extended to several miles beyond their encampment, leaving a neutral space unoccupied by either forces. Often reconnoitering parties would meet beyond the pickets and exchange shots, and often pickets were killed at their posts by an enemy slipping up through the bushes unaware to the victim. I always considered such as willful murder.

It became my time to go on picket; the post assigned to me was on the banks of the River, three miles beyond our camps. The night before one of our men was shot from across the River.

Usually three men were detailed to perform that duty, so that they can divide watch every two hours, one to guard and two to sleep, if such was possible. On that occasion the guard was doubled and six men were detailed, and while four lay on the ground in blankets, two were on the look-out. The post we picked out was under a very large oak; in our immediate rear was a corn field the corn of which was already appropriated by the cavalry. The field was surrounded by a low fence and the boys at rest lay in the fence corners. It was a bright starlight September night, no moon visible, but one could distinguish an object some distance beyond. I was on the watch. It was about eleven P. M., when through the still night, I heard foot-steps and the breaking of corn stalks. I listened intently, and the noise ceased. Presently I heard it again; being on the alert, and so was my fellow-watchman, we cautiously awoke the men who were happy in the arms of Morpheus, not even dreaming of any danger besetting their surroundings. I whispered to them to get ready quietly, that we heard the approach of someone walking in our front. The guns which were in reach beside them were firmly grasped. We listened and watched, in a stooping position, when the noise started again, yet a little

A Picket Shot While on Duty, Nothing
Short of Murder.

more pronounced and closer. We were ready to do our duty. I became impatient at the delay, and not wishing to be taken by surprise, I thought I would surprise somebody myself, so took my musket at a trail, crept along the fence to reconnoiter, while my comrades kept their position. When suddenly appeared ahead of me a white object, apparently a shirt bosom. I cocked my gun, but my target disappeared, and I heard a horse snorting. On close inspection, I found that it was a loose horse grazing, and what I took for a shirt bosom was his pale face, which sometimes showed, when erect, then disappeared while grazing. I returned and reported, to the great relief of us all. Heretofore, men on guard at the outpost would fire their guns on hearing any unusual noise and thus alarming the army, which at once would put itself in readiness for defense, only to find out that it was a false alarm and that they were needlessly disturbed. Such occurrences happened too often, therefore a general order was read that any man that would fire his gun needlessly and without good cause, or could not give a good reason for doing so would be court-martialed and dealt with accordingly. Therefore, the writer was especially careful not to violate these orders.

At another time it became again my lot to go on vidette duty. This time it was three miles in the opposite direction in the rear of the camp in the Allegheny, in a Northwesterly direction, in a perfect wilderness, an undergrowth of a virgin forest. It was a very gloomy evening the clouds being low. A continual mist was falling. It was in the latter part of September. We were placed in a depressed piece of ground surrounded by mountains. The detail consisted of Walker Knight, Alfred Barnes and myself. Corporal Renfroe, whose duty was to place us in position, gave us the following instructions and returned to camp: "Divide your time as usual, no fire allowed, shoot anyone approaching without challenge." Night was falling fast, and in a short while there was Egyptian darkness. We could not even see our hands before our eyes. There was a small spruce pine, the stem about five inches in diameter, with its limbs just above our heads. We placed ourselves under it as a protection from the mist, and in case it would rain. All at once, we heard a terrible yell, just such as a wild cat might send forth, only many times louder. This was answered it seemed like, from every direction. Barnes remarked "What in the world is that?" I said, "Panthers, it looks like the woods are full of them." The panthers, from what we learned from inhabitants are dangerous animals, and often attack man, being a feline species, they can see in the dark. I said, "There is no sleep for us, let us form a triangle, back to back against this tree, so in case of an attack, we are facing in every direction." Not being able to see, our guns and bayonets were useless, and we took our pocket knives in hand in case of an attack at close quarters. The noise of these beasts kept up a regular chorus all night long, and we would have preferred to meet a regiment of the enemy than to be placed in such a position. We were all young and inexperienced. I was the oldest, and not more than twenty-three years old. Walker Knight said, "Boys, I can't stand it any longer, I am going back to camp." I said, "Walker, would you leave your post to be court-martialed, and reported as a coward? Then, you would not find the way back, this dark night, and be torn up before you would get there. Here, we can protect each other." Occasionally we heard dry limbs on the ground, crack, as if someone walking on them. This was rather close quarters to be comfortable, especially when one could not see at all. There we stood, not a word was spoken above a whisper, when we heard a regular snarl close by, then Barnes

said, "What is that?" I said, "I expect it is a
bear." All this conversation was in the lowest
whisper; to tell the truth, it was the worst night
I ever passed, and my friend Knight, even now
says that he could feel his hair on his head stand
straight up.

My dear reader, don't you believe we were
glad when day broke on us? It was seemingly
the longest night I ever spent, and so say my
two comrades.

The country from Monterey to Cheat Mountain was not inhabited, with the exception of a
tavern on top of the Allegheny, where travelers might find refreshments for man and
beast. The enemy often harassed us with
scouting parties, and attacking isolated posts.
To check these maneuvres, we did the same;
so one evening, Lieutenant Dawson of the
Twelfth Georgia Regiment, Captain Willis
Hawkins' Company from Sumter County, and
which regiment formed a contingent part of our
forces at Green Brier River, came to me saying, "Hermann, I want you tonight." He was
a fearless scout, a kind of warfare that suited
his taste, and he always called on me on such
occasions. And after my last picket experience,
I was only too willing to go with him, as it

relieved me from army duty the day following, and I preferred that kind of excitement to standing guard duty.

We left at dark, and marched about four miles, towards the enemy's camp to Cheat River, a rather narrow stream to be a river. A wooden bridge spanned the stream. We halted this side. On our right was a steep mountain, the turn pike or road rounded it nearly at its base. The mountain side was covered with flat loose rocks of all sizes, averaging all kinds of thickness. By standing some on their edge, and propping them with another rock, afforded fine protection against minnie balls. In this manner we placed ourselves in position behind this improvised breastworks.

The mot d'ordre was not to fire until the command was given. We were ten in number, and the understanding was to fire as we lay, so as to hit as many as possible. At about ten o'clock P. M. we heard the enemy crossing the bridge, their horses's hoofs were muffled so as to make a noiseless crossing, and take our pickets by surprise. They came within fifty yards of us and halted in Column. Lieutenant Dawson commanded the man next to him to pass it up the line to make ready to shoot, when he commanded in a loud voice, "Fire!" Instantly, as per one crack of a musket, all of us fired, and consternation reigned among the enemy's ranks; those that could get away stampeded across the bridge. We did not leave our position until day. When we saw the way was clear, we gathered them up, took care of the wounded and buried the dead—several of our shots were effective. On the 3rd of October, they made an attack on us in full force, and while they drove in our picketc, we had ample time to prepare to give them a warm reception.

The following is a description of the battle ground and a description of our forces:

On the extreme right, in an open meadow, not far from the banks of the river, was the First Georgia Regiment, lying flat on the grass; to the immediate left and rear was a battery of four guns, on a mount immediately confronting the turn pike, and fortified by breastworks, and supported by the Forty-fourth Virginia Regiment, commanded by Colonel Scott; further to left, across the road was a masked battery, with abatis in front, Captain Anderson commanding, and supported by the Third Arkansas Regiment and the Twelfth Georgia Regiment, commanded by Colonels Rusk and

Johnston respectively. As the enemy came down the turn pike, the battery on our left, commanding that position, opened on them, the enemy from across the river responded with alacrity, and there was a regular artillery duel continuously. Their infantry filed to their left, extending their line beyond that of the First Georgia, they followed the edge of the stream at the foot of the mountain. We detached two Companies from the Regiment further to our right, to extend our line. They were not more than two hundred yards in front. The balance of the regiment lay low in its position; the order was to shoot low, and not before we could see the white of their eyes.

The enemy would fire on us continually, but the balls went over us and did no damage. While maneuvring thus on our right, they made a vigorous attack on Anderson's battery, but were repulsed with heavy loss. Late in the afternoon they withdrew. Our casualties were very small, and that of the enemy considerable.

Colonel Ramsey, who, early that morning went out on an inspection tour, dismounted for some cause, his horse came into camp without a rider, and we gave him up for lost, but later, a little before dark, he came in camp, to the great rejoicing of the regiment, for we all loved him. General Henry R. Jackson was our commander at that time, and soon afterwards was transferred South.

The enemy had all the advantage by the superiority of their arms, while ours were muzzle loaders, carrying balls but a very short distance; theirs were long range, hence we could not reach them only at close quarters. A very amusing instant was had during their desultory firing. The air was full of a strange noise; it did not sound like the hiss of a minnie-ball, nor like that of a cannon ball. It was clearly audible all along the line of the First Georgia; the boys could not help tucking their heads. The next day some of the men picked up a ram rod at the base of a tree where it struck broadside, and curved into a half circle. It was unlike any we had, and undoubtedly the fellow forgot to draw it out of the gun, fired it at us, and this was the strange sound we heard which made us dodge. A few nights later, a very dark night, we sent out a strong detachment, under Command of Colonel Talliaferro to cut off their pickets, which extended to Slavins Cabin (an old abandoned log house). To cross the river we put wagons in the run; a twelve inch plank connected the wagons and served as a bridge.

On the other side of the river was a torch bearer, holding his torch so that the men could see how to cross. The torch blinded me, and instead of looking ahead, I looked down. It seemed that the men with the torch shifted the light, casting the shadow of a connecting plank to the right, when instead of stepping on the plank, I stepped on the shadow, and down in the water I went (rather a cold bath in October) and before morning, my clothing was actually frozen. In crossing Cheat River Bridge, the road tacked to the left, making a sudden turn, which ran parallel with the same road under it. The head of the column having reached there, the rear thinking them to be enemies, fired into them. Haply no one was hurt before the mistake was discovered, but the enemy got notice of our approach by the firing, and had withdrawn, so the expedition was for naught. We were back in camp about eight o'clock the following morning.

At the latter end of the month Colonel Edward Johnson concluded to attack General Reynolds in his stronghold on Cheat Mountain.

The Third Arkansas Regiment, under command of Colonel Rusk, was detached and sent to the rear, taking a long detour a couple of days ahead, and making demonstrations, while the main force would attack them in front. Colonel Rusk was to give the signal for attack. Early in the night we sent out a large scouting party to attack their pickets, and drive them in. Lieutenant Dawson was in command. Early that day we started with all the forces up Cheat Mountain, a march of twelve miles. During the progress of our march the advance guard having performed what was assigned them to do, returned by a settlement road running parallel with the turn pike for some distance, when of a sudden, balls were hissing among us and some of the men were hit. The fire was returned at once, and flanker drawn out whose duty it was to march on the flank of the column, some twenty paces by its side, keeping a sharp lookout. I mistook the order, and went down into the woods as a scout, the firing still going on, and I was caught between them both. I hugged close to the ground keeping a sharp look-out to my right. When I recognized the Company's uniform, and some of my own men, I hollowed at them to stop firing, that they were shooting our own men, when they hollowed, "Hurrah for Jeff Davis," when from above, Colonel Johnson responded, "Damn lies, boys, pop it to them," when Weaver Jones stuck a white handkerchief on his bayonet and the firing ceased.

Sergeant P. R. Talliaferro was hit in the breast by a spent ball. Weaver had a lock of his hair just above his ear cut off as though it had been shaved off. One man was wounded and bled to death, another was wounded and recovered. Such mistakes happened often in our lines for the lack of sound military knowledge.

The man that bled to death was from the Dahlonega Guards. He said while dying, that he would not mind being killed by an enemy's bullet, but to be killed by his own friends is too bad. Everything was done that could be done for the poor fellow, but of no avail.

The column advanced to a plateau, overlooking the enemy's camp. We placed our guns in battery, waiting for the Rusk signal, which was never given; we waited until four o'clock P. M. and retraced our steps without firing a gun. We saw their lines of fortification and their flags flying from a bastion, but not a soul was visible. We thought Reynolds had given us the slip and that we would find him in our rear and in our camp before we could get back, so we double quicked at a fox trot, until we reached our quarters in the early part of the night.

Colonel Rusk came in two days afterward, and reported that his venture was impracticable.

Cold winter was approaching with rapid strides and rations were not to the entire satisfaction of our men. The beef that was issued to us, although very fine, had become a monotonous diet, and the men longed for something else, they had become satiated with it, so I proposed to Captain Jones that if he would report me accounted for in his report, that I would go over to Monterey and McDowell on a foraging expedition. and bring provisions for the Company. He said he would, but I must not get him into trouble, for the orders were that no permits be issued for anyone to leave camp and that all passes, if any be issued, must be countersigned by Captain Anderson, who was appointed Commander of the post. We still were without tents for they were captured by the enemy at Carricks Ford, and we sheltered ourselves the best we could with the blankets we had received from home. The snow had fallen during the night to the depth of eight inches, and it was a strange sight to see the whole camp snowed under, (literally speaking). When morning approached, the writer while not asleep, was not entirely aroused. He lay there under his blanket, a gentle perspiration was oozing from every pore of his skin, when suddenly, he aroused himself, and rose up.

Not a man was to be seen, the hillocks of snow, however, showed where they lay, so I hollowed, "look at the snow." Like jumping out of the graves, the men pounced up in a jiffy, they were wrestling and snowballing and rubbing each other with it. After having performed all the duties devolving upon me that afternoon, I started up the Allegheny where some members of my Company with others, were detailed, building winter quarters. Every carpenter in the whole command was detailed for that purpose.

CHAPTER VIII.

When some three miles beyond camps, I noted a little smoke arising as I approached. I noted that it was the outpost. My cap was covered with an oil cloth, and I had an overcoat with a cape, such as officers wore; hence the guard could not tell whether I was a private, corporal or a general. I noticed that they had seen me approach. One of them advanced to the road to challenge me, but I spoke first. I knew it was against the orders to have a fire at the outpost on vidette duty so I said, "Who told you to have a fire? Put out that fire, sirs, don't you know it is strictly prohibited?"—"What is your name—what Company do you belong to, and what is your regiment?" all of which was answered. I took my little note book and pencil, and made an entry, or at least made a bluff in this direction, and said, "You'll hear from me again." I had the poor fellow scared pretty badly, and they never even made any demand on me to find out who I was. They belonged to Colonel Scott's regiments. The bluff worked like a charm, and I marched on. When about six miles from camp, I was pretty tired, walking in the snow and up-hill. I saw General

Henry R. Jackson, and Major B. L. Blum, coming along in a jersey wagon. The General asked me where I was going,—it was my time to get a little scared. I answered that I was going on top the Allegheny where they built winter quarters. "Get in the wagon, you can ride, we are going that way." I thanked them; undoubtedly the General thought that I was detailed to go there and to assist in that work. This is the last I saw of General Jackson in that country.

Among the men I found Tom Tyson, Richard Hines, William Roberson (surnamed "Crusoe"). I spent the night with them in a cabin they had built and the following morning I took an early start down the mountain toward Monterey. It had continued to snow all the night and it lay to the depth of twelve inches. I could only follow the road by the opening distance of the tree tops, and which sometimes was misleading. I passed the half-way house, known as the tavern, about 9 o'clock A. M. Four hundred yards beyond, going in an oblique direction at an angle of about 45 degrees, I saw a large bear going through the woods; he was a fine specimen, his fur was as black as coal. I approximate his size as about between three hundred and four hundred pounds. He turned his head and looked at me and stopped. I at once halted, bringing my musket to a trail. I was afraid to fire for fear of missing my mark, my musket being inaccurate, so I reserved my fire for closer quarters, the bear being at least fifty yards from me, and he followed his course in a walk. I was surprised and said to myself, —"Old fellow, if you let me alone, I surely will not bother you."

I watched him 'till he was out of my sight. My reason for not shooting him was two-fold; first, I was afraid I might miss him, and my gun being a muzzle loader, the distance between us was too short, and he would have been on me before I could have reloaded, so I reserved my fire, expecting to get in closer proximity. I was agreeably surprised when he continued his journey. When I came to Monterey that afternoon, I told some of its citizens what a narrow escape I had. They smiled and said "Bears seldom attack human, unless in very great extremities, but I did well not to have shot unless I was sure that I would have killed him, for a wounded bear would stop the flow of blood with his fur, by tapping himself on the wound, and face his antagonist, and I could have been sure he would have gotten the best of me."

From Monterey I went over to McDowell, fourteen miles, to see my friend Eagle and his brother-in-law, Sanders, he that made the twelve Yankees run by running in front of them. I stated my business and invoked their assistance, which they cheerfully extended. In about three days we had about as much as a four horse team could pull.

Provisions sold cheap. One could buy a fine turkey for fifty cents, a chicken for fifteen to twenty cents, butter twelve and one-half cents and everything else in proportion. Apples were given me for the gathering of them. Bacon and hams for seven to eight cents per pound, the finest cured I ever tasted.

The people in these regions lived bountifully, and always had an abundance to spare. Mr. Eagle furnished the team and accompanied me to camp, free of charge. Money was a scarce article at that time among the boys; the government was several months in arrear with our pay, but we expected to be paid off daily, so Mr. Eagle said he would be responsible to the parties that furnished the provisions, and the Company could pay him when we got our money; he was one of the most liberal and patriotic men that it was my pleasure to meet during the war.

Four days later, Captain Jones received our money. I kept a record of all the provisions furnished to each man, and the captain deducted the amount from each. I wrote Eagle to come up and get his money; he came, and received every cent that was due him.

But I must not omit an incident that occurred when near our camp with the load of provisions. I had to pass hard by the Twelfth Georgia Regiment, which was camped on the side of the turnpike, when some of the men who were as anxious for a change of diet as we were, came to me and proposed to buy some of my provisions. I stated that they were sold and belonged to Company E, First Regiment, and that I could not dispose of them. Some Smart-Aleks, such as one may find among any gathering of men, proposed to charge the wagon and appropriate its contents by force. Seeing trouble ahead, I drew my pistol, when about a dozen men ran out with their guns. Eagle turned pale, he thought his time had come, when a Lieutenant interfered, asking the cause of the disturbance, which I stated. He said, "Men, none of that, back with those guns." He mounted the wagon and accompanied us to my camp, which was a few hundred yards beyond.

CHAPTER IX.

Once later, I was called out for fatigue duty. I said, "Corporal, what is to be done?" He answered, "To cut wood for the blacksmith shop." I replied, "You had better get someone else who knows how, I never cut a stick in my life," he said, "You are not too old to learn how." This was conclusive, so he furnished me with an axe, and we marched into the woods, and he said he would be back directly with a wagon to get the wood and he left me. I was looking about me to find a tree, not too large, one that I thought I could manage. I spied a sugar maple about eight inches in diameter. I sent my axe into it, but did not take my cut large enough to reach the center, when it came down to a feather edge and I did not have judgment enough to know how to enlarge my cut by cutting from above, so I started a new cut from the right, another from the left, bringing the center to a pivot of about three inches in diameter, as solid as the Rock of Gibraltar; finally, by continuous hacking, I brought it to a point where I could push it back and forth. The momentum finally broke the center, but in place of falling, the top lodged in a neighboring tree, and I could not dislodge it. I worked hard, the perspiration ran down my face, my hands were lacerated, I finally got mad, and sent the axe a-glimmering, and it slid under the snow. After awhile my corporal came for the wood; "Where is the wood?" I showed him the tree; "Is that all you have done?" I could not restrain any longer, I said, "Confound you, I told you I did not know anything about cutting wood." "Where is the axe?". we looked everywhere but could not find it; it must have slid under the snow and left no trace, so he arrested me and conducted me before Colonel Edward Johnson, a West Pointer, in command of the post. He was at his desk writing; turning to face us, he addressed himself to me, who stood there, cap in hand, while the Corporal stood there with his kept on his head. "What can I do for you?" I said, looking at the Corporal. "He has me under arrest and brought me here." Looking at the corporal the Colonel said, "Pull off your hat, sir, when you enter officers' quarters." (I would not have taken a dollar for that). The Corporal pulled off his cap. "What have you arrested him for?" The Corporal answered that I was regularly detailed to cut wood for the blacksmith shop, and that I failed to do my duty, and lost the axe he furnished me. "Why did you not cut the wood?" said the Colonel. "I tried," said I, "I told him that I had never cut any wood and did not know how; where I came from there are no woods. Look at my hands." They were badly blistered and lacerated. The Colonel cursed out the Corporal as an imbecile, for not getting someone who was used to such work. I told the Colonel how hard I had tried and what I had done. The Colonel smiled and said, "What did you do with the axe?"; "When the tree lodged and I could not budge it, I got mad and made a swing or two with the axe, and let her slide; it must have slid under the snow, and we could not find it." "What have you done for a living?" "After I quit school, I clerked in a store." "Can you write?" "Oh, yes!" "Let me see." "My hand is too sore and hurt now." "Well, come around tomorrow, I may get you a job here."

Next day I called at his quarters, and he put me to copying some documents and reports, which I did to his satisfaction. I had warm quarters and was relieved from camp duties for a little while.

This brings us to about the middle of December, and we were ordered to Winchester. Colonel Johnson with his Regiment and a small force, was left in charge of the Winter Quarters on the Allegheny, so I took leave of him to join my Company.

Colonel Johnson, while a little brusk in his demeanor, was a clever, social gentleman, and a good fighter, which he proved to be when the enemy made a night descent on him and took him by surprise. He rallied his men, barefooted in the snow, knee-deep, thrashed out the enemy and held the fort; he was promoted to General and was afterwards known as the Allegheny Johnson.

My Command having preceded me, I went to Staunton, where I met J. T. Youngblood, Robert Parnelle and others from my Company. I also met Lieutenant B. D. Evans of my Company, just returned from a visit from home. We took the stage coach from Stanton to Winchester through Kanawah Valley. We passed Woodstock, Strasburg, New Market, Middletown, and arrived at Winchester in due time. General T. J. Jackson in command, we had a splendid camp about a mile to the left of the city. The weather had greatly moderated and the snow was melting. The regiment had received tents to which we built chimneys with flat rocks that were abundant all around us. The flour barrels served as chimney stacks, and we were comfortable; rations were also good and plentiful, but hardly were we installed when we received orders to strike camps. The men were greatly disappointed; we expected to be permitted to spend winter there. We took up the line of march late in the evening, marched all night and struck Bath early in the morning, took the enemy by surprise while they were fixing their morning meal, which they left, and the boys regaled themselves. The Commissary and Quartermaster also left a good supply behind in their rapid flight, and we appropriated many provisions, shoes, blankets and overcoats; from Bath we marched to Hancock, whipped out a small force of the enemy, and continued our force to Romney where we struck camps. Romney is a small town situated on the other side of the Potomac River. General Jackson demanded the surrender of the place, the enemy refused, so he ordered the non-combatants to leave, as he would bombard the town. Bringing up a large cannon which we called "Long Tom" owing to its size, he fired one round and ordered us to fall back. All this was during Christmas week.

On our return it turned very cold and sleeted;

the road became slick and frozen, and not being prepared for the emergency, I saw mules, horses and men take some of the hardest falls, as we retraced our steps, the road being down grade. This short campaign was a success and accomplished all it intended from a military standpoint, although we lost many men from exposure; pneumonia was prevalent among many of our men. We have now returned to Winchester. The writer himself, at that time, thought that this campaign was at a great sacrifice of lives from hardships and exposures, but later on, learned that it was intended as a check to enable General Lee in handling his forces against an overwhelming force of the enemy, and being still reinforced and whose battle cry still was "On to Richmond." It was for this reason that General "Stonewall" Jackson threatened Washington via Romney and the enemy had to recall their reinforcements intended against General Lee to protect Washington.

The men from the Southern States were not used to such rigorous climate and many of our men had to succumb from exposure. My Company lost three men from pneumonia, viz:— Sam and Richard Hines, two splendid soldiers, and brothers, and Lorenzo Medlock. The writer also was incapacitated. There were no preparations in Winchester for such contingencies, so the churches were used as hospitals. The men were packed in the pews wrapped in their blankets, others were lying on the nasty humid floor, for it must be remembered that the streets in Winchester were perfect lobbies of dirt and snow tramped over by men, horses and vehicles. While there in that condition I had the good fortune to be noted by one of my regiment, he was tall and of herculean form, his name was Griswold, and while he and myself on a previous occasion had some misunderstanding and therefore not on speaking terms, he came to me and extended his hand, saying: "Let us be friends, we have hard times enough without adding to it." I was too sick to talk, but extended my hand, in token of having buried the hatchet. He asked me if he could do anything for me. I shook my head and shut my eyes. I was very weak. When I opened them he was gone. During the day he returned, saying: "I found a better place for you at a private house. He wrapped me in my blanket and carried me on his shoulders a distance of over three blocks. Mrs. Mandelbawm, the lady of the house, had a nice comfortable room prepared for me, and Griswold waited on me like a brother, he was a powerful man, but very overbearing at times, but had a good heart. Mr. Mandelbawm sent their family physician, who prescribed for me. He pronounced me very sick, he did not know how it might terminate. It took all his efforts and my determination to get well after three weeks struggling to accomplish this end. My friend came to see me daily when off duty.

The regiment's term of enlistment will soon have expired, for we only enlisted for one year. The regiment received marching order, not being strong enough for duty. Through the recommendation of my doctor and regimental color, I was discharged and sent home. The regiment had been ordered to Tennessee, but owing to a wreck on the road they were disbanded at Petersburg, Va., and the boys arrived home ten days later than I.

In getting my transportation the Quartermaster asked me to deliver a package to General Beaureguard as I would pass via Manassas Junction. When I arrived I inquired for his quarters, when I was informed that he had left for Centreville, I followed to that place, when I was told he had left for Richmond. Arriving at Richmond I went at once to the Executive Department in quest of him and should I fail to find him, would leave my package there, which I did. This was on Saturday evening, I had not a copper in money with me, but I had my pay roll; going at once to the Treasury Department, to my utter consternation, I found it closed. A very affable gentlemen informed me that the office was closed until Monday morning. I said, "What am I to do, I have not a cent of money in my pocket and no baggage," for at that time hotels had adopted a rule that guests without baggage would have to pay in advance. I remarked that I could not stay out in the streets, so the gentleman pulled a $10.00 bill out of his pocket and handed it to me saying, "Will that do you until Monday morning, 8 o'clock? When the office will be open, everything will be all right." I thanked him very kindly. Monday I presented my bill which was over six months in arrears. They paid it at once in Alabama State bills, a twenty-five cent silver and two cents coppers. I did not question the correctness of their calculation. I took the money and went in quest of my friend who so kindly advanced me the $10.00. I found him sitting at a desk. He was very busy. I handed him a $10.00 bill and again thanked him for his kindness; he refused it saying: "Never mind, you are a long ways from home and may need it." I replied that I had enough to make out without it, I said that I appreciated it, but didn't like to take presents from strangers; he said, "We are no strangers, my name is Juda P. Benjamin." Mr. Benjamin was at that time Secretary of the Treasury of the Confederate States. He was an eminent lawyer from the State of Louisiana, he became later on Secretary of War, and when Lee surrendered he escaped to England to avoid the wrath of the Federal Officials who offered a premium for his capture. He became Queen's Consul in England and his reputation became international. No American who was stranded ever appealed to him in vain, especially those from the South. It is said of him that he gave away fortunes in charity.

I came back to Georgia among my friends who were proud to see me. Having no near relations, such as father or mother, sisters or brothers to welcome me, as had my comrades, my friends all over the County took pride in performing that duty, and thus ended my first year's experience as a soldier in the war between the States.

CHAPTER X.

Notwithstanding the arduous campaign and severe hardships endured during my first year's service, I did not feel the least depressed in spirit or patriotism. On the contrary the arms of the Confederacy in the main had proven themselves very successful in repelling the enemy's attacks and forcing that government continually to call new levees to crush our forces in the field.

Those measures on the part of our adversaries appealed to every patriot at home and regardless of hardships already endured. Hence the First Georgia Regiment although disbanded as an organization, the rank and file had sufficient pluck to re-enter the service for the period of the war regardless as to how long it might last. Possessing some hard endured experience, many of them organized commands of their own, or joined other commands as subalterns or commissioned officers.

The following is a roll of promotion from the members of the Washington Rifles as first organized.—See Appendix D.

The foregoing record proves that the Washington Rifles were composed of men capable of handling forces and that it had furnished men

WAR BETWEEN THE STATES 73

and officers in every branch of service in the Confederate States Army, and had been active after their return home from their first year's experience in raising no little army themselves, and what I have recorded of the Washington Rifles may be written of every Company composing the First Georgia Regiment.

The State of Georgia furnished more men than any other State, and Washington County furnished more Companies than any other County in the State.

Such men cannot be denominated as rebels or traitors, epithets that our enemies would fain have heaped upon us. If the true history of the United States as written before the war and adopted in every school-house in the land, North, South, East and West, did not demonstrate them as patriots, ready and willing to sacrifice all but honor on the altar of their country.

On the first of May, 1862, Sergeant E. P. Howell came to me saying: "Herman, how would you like to help me make up an artillery Company? I have a relative in South Carolina who is a West Pointer and understands that branch of the service. The Yankees are making tremendous efforts for new levees and we, of the South, have to meet them." "All right," said I, "I am tired after my experience with infantry, having gone through with 'Stonewall's' foot cavalry in his Romney campaign." The following day we made a tour in the neighborhood and enlisted a few of our old comrades in our enterprise. We put a notice in the Herald, a weekly paper edited by J. M. G. Medlock, that on the 10th day of May we would meet in Sandersville for organization, and then and there we formed an artillery Company that was to be known as the Sam Robinson Artillery Company, in honor of an old and venerable citizen of our County.

General Robinson, in appreciation of our having named the Company in his honor presented the organization with $1,000.00, which money was applied in uniforming us.

The following members formed the composite of said Company, and Robert Martin, known as "Bob Martin" from Barnwell, S. C., was elected Captain. See appendix E.

The writer was appointed bugler with rank of Sergeant.

That night after supper, it being moon-light, Mr. A. J. Linville a North Carolinian, a school teacher boarding at my lodging proposed to me as I performed on the flute, he being a violinist, to have some music on the water. He then explained that water is a conductor of sound and that one could hear playing on it for a long distance and music would sound a great deal sweeter and more melodious than on land. The Ogeechee River ran within a couple of hundred yards from the house. There was on the bank and close to the bridge a party of gentlemen fishing, having a large camp fire and prepared to have a fish-fry, so Linville and myself took a boat that was moored above the bridge and quietly, unbeknown to anybody paddled about 1 1-4 mile up stream, expecting to float down with the current. Although it was the month of May the night was chilly enough for an overcoat. Linville and myself struck up a tune, allowing the boat to float along with the current, the oar laying across my lap. Everything was lovely, the moon was shining bright and I enjoyed the novelty of the surroundings and the music, when an over-hanging limb of a tree struck me on the neck. Wishing to disengage myself, I gave it a shove, and away went the boat from under me and I fell backwards into the stream in 12 feet of water. To gain the surface I had to do some hard kicking, my boots having filled with water and my heavy overcoat kept me weighted down.

When reaching the surface after a hard struggle my first observation was for the boat which was about 50 yards below, Linville swinging to a limb. I called him to meet me, and he replied that he had no oar, that I kicked it out of the boat. The banks on each side were steep and my effecting a landing was rather slim. I spied a small bush half-way up the embankment, I made for it perfectly exhausted, I grabbed it, the bank was too steep and slippery to enable me to land, so I held on and rested and managed to disembarrass myself of the overcoat and told Linville to hold on, that I was coming. I could not get my boots off, so I made an extra effort to reach him anyhow, as the current would assist me by being in my favor, so I launched off. I reached the boat perfectly worn out. I do not think I could have made another stroke. After a little breathing spell and by a tremendous effort I hoisted myself into the boat, but not before it dipped some water.

On our way I picked up my discarded overcoat and a piece of a limb which served as a rudder to guide the boat to a successful landing, and thus ended the music on the water.

We went to the house, changed our clothes and returned, mingling with the fishermen and kept all the fun we had to ourselves. They all made a fine catch and there was fish a plenty for all. Linville and myself enjoyed the repast, as the physical exercise we had just undergone sharpened our appetite.

A few days later we rendezvoued at Sandersville, and the Company left for Savannah, our camp of instruction. Under the tuition of Jacobi, leader of the band of the 32nd Georgia, W. H. Harrison's Regiment, I soon learned all the calls and commands.

While thus engaged the Company had a gross misunderstanding with Capt. Martin, who, before coming in contact with the members of his command, was an entire stranger to them. Most all were ignorant of military duties, but strictly honest and patriotic citizens. Capt. Martin was a strict disciplinarian and putting the screws on rather a little too tight placed him into disfavor with the men, who petitioned him to resign, otherwise they would prefer charges against him. Thus matters stood when I returned to camp. Martin was tried before a board and exonerated. To revenge himself upon those who were active in his persecution he reduced those that were non-commissioned officers to ranks and appointed others in their stead; and to make matters more galling, appointed a substitute, a mercenary as orderly

Sergeant over a Company of volunteers, who solely served their country through patriotism. Ned Irwin, when elevated to the position he was, proved himself a worthy tool in the hand of his promoter. Men could not express an opinion on hardly any subject without being reported, he would sneak about in the dark, crouch behind a tent evesdropping and make report as unfavorably as he could to bring the individual into disfavor. He made himself so obnoxious that he did not have a friend in the whole Company, and when he died at Yazoo City, you could hear freely expressed the following sentiment: "Poor old Ned is dead, thank God this saves some good men of having to kill him."

When I returned to camp I presented myself before Capt. Martin who examined me as to my proficiency as a bugler. I said, "Captain, there has been quite some changes made since I have been away," he said, "Yes, the men have accused me of speculating on their rations." I said I was very sorry that such a state of affairs existed among officers and men, where harmony ought to prevail; he said he insisted that those charges be substantiated and demanded a court martial, who on hearing the facts cleared him of any criminality, so he punished the leaders of the gang by reducing them to ranks.

Capt. Martin, however, proved himself a capable officer in handling artillery and the men finally came to love him on account of his efficiency and fairness.

While in camp of instructions in Savannah, the Government furnished us with six brass pieces (2 Howitzer and 4 Napoleon) with the necessary accoutrement and horses and we were ordered to Bryan County in support of Fort McAllister. We went into camp by the side of the Ogeechee River, about three miles this side of the Fort, which camp we named "Camp McAllister." The fort was an earth structure, strongly constructed with redoubts and parapets. The magazine underground was strongly protected by heavy timbers, and so was what we called bomb-proof, for the men not actually engaged, but who were ready to relieve those who were, or became disabled under fire and exposure, and compelled to be at their post of duty. Short reliefs were necessary, for it is hard work to manage heavy seige guns, but the heaviest in that fort were only of forty-two caliber. For some time nothing of importance worth to chronicle happened; the boys attended to their regular camp life duty, roll calls and drills; those off duty went fishing along the river banks.

The country surrounding was low, flat, marshy and replete with malarial fever, so that we had to remove our camp several miles further up the river, but still within close call of the fort. This new camp was called "Camp Arnold," in honor of Doctor Arnold, on whose land we stationed. One morning I was ordered to blow the call, only one man, Sergeant Cox, reported. All the rest of the command were down with chills and fever. There was no quinine to be had, owing to the blockade, such medicines being considered by our adversaries as contraband of war. Men tried every remedy possible, even drank cottonseed tea, at the suggestion of a country physician by the name of Dr. Turner, who pronounced it as a good substitute (it was in taste if not in efficiency). The writer was also stricken with the disease, and was sent to Whitesville Hospital, about thirty miles from Savannah on the Central of Georgia Railroad. Dr. Whitehead was in charge of the same, and Madam Cazzier and her daughter from New Orleans were matrons. During my fever spells I would rave sometimes and not having been in this country over three years in all, my friends predominated over the English language. Madam Cazzier, who spoke French also, took a great interest in me; in fact, she was strictly interested in all the patients, but she seemed to be a little partial to myself, and spent some time by my bedside when the fever was off, and would tell me what I said during my delirium. She nursed me and devoted on me a motherly care, for which I shall always remain thankful. My recuperation was rapid, and I soon felt myself again.

One morning it was announced that General Mercer of Savannah, and the Board of Inspectors were to come on a round of inspection, when we heard heavy firing, the sounds coming from the east. Presently we heard that the enemy with a large fleet was attacking Fort McAllister. General Mercer and his Board had come up from Savannah on a special train. He called for all convalescent, able to fight to volunteer to go to the front. I presented myself; I was the only one. We cut loose the locomotive and one car and went flying to Savannah at the rate of a mile a minute, crossed the City in a buss at full speed to the Gulf Depot, now known as the S. F. & W., just in time to board the train to Way Station, twelve miles from Savannah. An ambulance carried us to the

Fort; the whole distance from the hospital to the Fort was about fifty-two miles. We changed conveyances three times and arrived at destination in less than two hours. Capt. Martin was in charge of a Mortar Detachment, so I reported to him for duty, but my place had been taken, and the detachment was complete, hence he had no use for me. I learned that Major Galley, the Commander of the Fort, had been killed by the first shot from the enemy's guns, which penetrated a sixteen foot embankment, knocked off the left hand trunnion of a thirty-two pounder, and struck the Major above the ear, and took off the top of his head, so Captain Anderson, of the Savannah Blues, took command. Captain Martin sent me up the River to a band about half a mile to the rear, which position placed me at a triangle point to the Fort and the gun boats. I was instructed to notice the effect of our shots on the enemy's boats. I kept tally sheets as to the hits between the belligerent points. From my observation I counted seventy-five hits by the guns of the Fort, and one hundred and seventy-five hits by those of the boats, which raised a cloud of dust equal to an explosion of a mine. Their caliber being three hundred and seventy-five pounders, and fifteen inches in diameter, while our shots merely made a bright spot where they struck the heavy armoured vessels and ricochet beyond. While thus observing I noted a strange move of one of the boats, suddenly I saw an immense flash, and a splash in the river a couple of yards in front of me. The water being very clear, we noted a large projective at the bottom of the stream, evidently aimed at me, as it was in direct line, as I sat on my horse; undoubtedly they must have taken me for a commanding officer and thus paid me their res— I mean disrespect.

A concourse of people in the neighborhood gathered to observe this unequal artillery duel of five armoured gun boats and eleven wooden mortar boats hidden behind a point below the Fort, sending their projectiles like a shower of aerolites into and around the Fort. Undaunted, the boys stood by their guns, having the satisfaction to notice one of the armoured vessels break their line and floating down the River, evidently having been struck in some vital part, and thus placed hors de combat. This bombardment continued from early morning until near sundown, when the enemy withdrew, we giving them parting shots as they steamed down to their blockade station, lying in wait for the Nashville, a blockade runner, who plyed between Nassau, and any Confederate Port, which it might enter with goods, easily disposed of at remunerative prices. The Fort was badly dilapidated, our breast-works had been blown to atoms, the guns exposed to plain view, all port holes demolished, the barracks injured by fire, which the boys extinguished while the battle was raging; in fact, had a cyclone struck the Fort in its full majestic force, it could not have been worse. However, that night we pressed into service all the negroes on the rice plantations. Spades, shovels and pick axes were handled with alacrity; baskets, bags and barrels were filled, the enfeebled portions of the Fort were reinforced by working like Trojans all night long, and the Fort was again placed in a presentable condition.

Early the following morning, when the enemy again appeared, undoubtedly to take possession, as the Fort would have been untenable in the condition they left it the previous evening, we opened fire on them, but they had seen what had been done during the night, saw at once that we were not disposed to give up; they withdrew without even returning our fire, and the boys would remark, they are treating us with silent contempt.

For awhile we enjoyed repose and the luxuries of the season at the Southern sea-coast, hunting squirrels, rabbits and fishing, getting leave of absence to visit home for a few days, when one day the report reached us that the enemy effected a landing at Killkanee, some distance below us and to our right. The battery was called out and we took up the line of march to meet the enemy. We camped that night near a church, when we were informed that the enemy's demonstration was against a small salt works, an enterprising citizen having erected a small furnace with a half a dozen boilers, in which he boiled sea water to obtain salt, which, at that time, was selling at a dollar a pound by the hundred pound sack. The Company returned to camp.

About ten days later word came late one afternoon that the enemy is making for Pocotalico, a small station on the Savannah and Charleston Railroad, intending to burn a long range of trestle on said road. Two detachments were sent to that place by post haste, arriving in time to place themselves in position, in as quiet a way as possible. At about ten o'clock P. M. we heard a very noisy demonstration to our right, through the marshes of the swamps; many torches became visible. They undoubtedly expected the place to be unprotected; when they came within full range we sent canister and schrapanel into the ranks; they fell back in confusion, leaving dead and wounded behind. This expedition started out from Beauford, S. C., then in possession of the enemy. One dark night the tide being up, the Nashville loaded with cotton attempted to run the gauntlet of the blockaders. On the turn of the river just opposite the Fort, the River Ogechee being about a mile wide, the vessel run aground on a sand bank, and was unable to extricate itself. The enemy being on the lookout, spied her position and came within firing distance; the Fort fired at them furiously, but they paid no attention to us, but concentrated their fire on the steamer Nashville with hot shots and soon had her in flames. The crew jumped overboard and swam ashore like ducks. The steamer was burned and completely destroyed. I was again taken with chills and fever and sent home by way of Dr. Whitehead's hospital. Sergeant Hines also came home to recuperate, when one morning I suggested to have an egg-nog. Cousin Abe was a merchant before the war, and still kept a store at Fenns Bridge, but the store had but few remnants in it. He only kept such goods as people were willing to dispose of in the way of exchange, for something else, and among his stock, he had a barrel of corn whiskey. I said, "Bill, if you furnish the eggs, I will furnish the sugar and whiskey; my chill will be on at eleven o'clock; we have an hour yet and kill or cure, I'm going to drink nog. It may help me." Dr. Whitehead had supplied me with a vial of Fowler's Solution, which was nearly exhausted, and which had done me no good. Sergeant Hines came up, brought a dozen eggs and we made a nog. At ten thirty A. M. I took the first goblet, he made it tolerably strong. I replenished and enjoyed the contents, and as we were sipping it quietly, I looked at my watch and was surprised to see it was fiften minutes past eleven and no chill. We slowly finished the third glass, I felt the effects of it somewhat, but we were not intoxicated. At twelve o'clock the dinner bell rang at the house, and it was the first time in two weeks that I was able to partake of that meal, the chills always interfering. I never had another chill in twenty years thereafter, hence I never became a prohibitionist. I believe the abuse of whiskey is wrong, while its proper use is right. Sergeant Hines and myself, after a few days longer among our friends, returned to our camp.

CHAPTER XI.

The following incident caused a rupture of friendship between Lieutenant Evan P. Howell and myself, which made military service unnecessarily harder on me, owing to our respective ranks. One night, it was on a Saturday, I had occasion to get up, it was late. I passed the sentinel on post number one, and recognized William Tolson on duty. I passed the usual greeting of "Hello! Bill, how do you do," "O, Ike, I'm so sick. I've one of the hardest chills on me I ever had." "Why don't you call the Corporal of the Guard, and get relief?" He replied, he wished I would call him, so I called "Corporal of the Guard, post number one." Corporal William O'Quinn came up to see what's up. I said, "Corporal, Tolson is sick and ought to be relieved." Presently the Corporal returned from headquarters, saying the officers are all gone over to Patterson, they were having a dance at the Quartermaster's, Major Cranston, and there is no one at headquarters but Dr. Stevenson who is drunk, and I can't get any sense out of him. When I told him that one of the men were sick, he said "You see that puppy, is he not the finest you have ever seen?" having reference to a small dog he fondled. "Finding out that I can't get any relief, I came back, so I told Tolson to go in and I would stand guard in his place. Tolson was a good soldier, he was a native Englishman, and when he got over his chill he was loud in his denunciation as to his treatment, so he was punished for having spoken derogatory about the officers and condemned to wear ball and chain for twenty-four hours. This was the first time that I knew there was such a thing as a ball and chain in camp for the punishment of man. The following Monday night, the writer having found out all about the particulars and the doings at the Quartermaster's, wrote up a program of intoxication at Granston Hall, Saturday night, March 1863. I treated the matter more of a burlesque than otherwise, and wound up in these words: "That's the way Confederate whiskey goes, pop goes the Government." Captain Martin was off and Lieutenant Howell was in command. Lieutenants Bland and Roberson laughed over the matter and took it good naturedly. W. N. Harmon was the only man in the Company who saw me write the article, and when finished I read it to him. He pronounced it a good joke and asked me what I was going to do with it. I said, "I am going to stick it up on the big pine where general orders are posted, so that the men can read it after reveille call, so he made some light-wood pegs, and we went together and posted it. The article was not signed, and was written in a round handwriting. The men enjoyed it and laughed a great deal over it, when Sergeant Fulford came up and tore down the paper, and carried it to the officer's tent. They inquired, what is the matter, what are the men laughing about. He presented the paper. Lieutenant Howell, after reading it, got raving mad, while Lieutenants Roberson and Bland took it good naturedly. Lieutenant Howell was determined to find out the author, so during the day he took up the men by fours and swore them on the Bible, if they knew who wrote the paper. I was at the station on that day and was absent. When I returned to my mess, they told me what was going on, and that Lieutenant Howell was trying to find out who wrote that article, so I said, "Bill," meaning William Harmon, "He took up the wrong men; if he had called on me I would have saved him that trouble". He answered, "Well, what will you do?" "Well, you don't believe that I would swear to a lie?" I got up saying, "I will satisfy his curiosity," and up to his tent I went. He was sitting in a chair smoking. "Good evening Lieutenant," says I. "I understand that you are very anxious to know who wrote that paper Sergeant Fulford submitted for your inspection. I can give you all the information you require." Lieutenant Howell at once brightened up and became all smiles. "You know—who did it?" "Your humble servant." In a twinkling his countenance changed. He became pale with rage, working himself into a passion, and very peremptorily ordered me to stand at attention. I at once planted my heels together to form a perfect angle, placed my little fingers along the seams of my pantaloons, my arms extending at full length, my body erect, facing my superior officer. I humbly remarked, "Will that do?"—"What did you do it for?"—"You had your fun, am I not entitled to have some?"—"You made false charges; you said we drank Government whiskey. I want you to understand what liquor we drank we bought and paid for it." "Well, Lieutenant, I have not accused anybody; not even mentioned a single name, but if the cap fits you, you can wear it. I have nothing to retract." By that time, Howell was surely mad. "I-I-I reduce you to ranks! I put you on double duty for thirty days and to wear ball and chain." "Is that all?" "Lieutenant, I volunteered in the Confederate army to do my full duty, as I always have done, in regard to duty; you only can put me on every other day, but when it comes to degrading me by making me wear ball and chain, I give you fair notice that I will kill any man who attempts to place the same on my limbs," and I made my exit, going to my mess-mates. "Well, how did you come out?" the boys asked me. I related what had passed between Lieutenant and I. William Harmon, then said, "Did you tell him that I helped you stick it up?" I said, "No, I shouldered the whole responsibility. What good would it do to implicate you?" "Well you shall not be the only one to do double duty," and off he went to tell Lieutenant Howell that he also had a hand in it, and consequently he was also condemned to double duty for thirty days. "Did he also tell you to wear ball and chain?" Harmon said "No."

That night, I slept, as the saying is, with one eye open. I had my pistol within easy reach, and my sabre by my side. No attempt however, was made to chain me. The following morning I was called for guard duty. I took my post, carrying my sabre across my neck, bear fashion. My post was in full view of the officers' headquarters. When Lieutenant Howell sent Sergeant Hines to me to tell me if I didn't carry my sabre at "Carry Sabre," he would keep me on four hours instead of two. Having been the bugler of the Company I was never instructed how to carry sabre. "Sergeant, can't you teach me how?" Hines remarked, "I know you know better how to handle a sabre than anyone in camp. I have seen you and Hoffman fight at Laurel Hill. I tell you, I have been on duty all night and I would like to go to sleep. This may be fun to you, but not to me, just now." I said, "Well Bill, go ahead," so I carried my sword to suit his Excellency, the commanding officer.

Later in the day J. J. Sheppard came to me saying, "Ike, Lieutenant Howell told me that I was appointed bugler in your place." "Well, sir, I congratulate you on your promotion." "He said for me to ask you for the bugle." I said, "All right Sheppard," I took the bugle and broke it in halves and handed it to Sheppard. He looked astonished—I remarked, "That instrument is private property and belongs to me, my money paid for it, and I have a right to handle it as I please, not meaning any disrespect to you, Sheppard." The following day, word came in camp for volunteers to handle siege pieces in Charleston, S. C. The enemy making heavy demonstration against that City. The Company sent men they could spare, among whom I formed a contingent part. My detachment was placed in the battery in charge of a heavy siege gun. The people of that City treated us royally and brought us plenty of provisions besides what we got from the commissary. We remained there a couple of weeks. The whole business turned out to be a fiasco, and we returned back to our camps. It was one of the most pleasant periods I have enjoyed during the whole war. I was again called on duty when I remarked, "This comes around pretty often." The Sergeant remarked, "You have to finish your sentence." I at once went to headquarters and met Lieutenant Howell and said, "Do you intend to make me finish the penalty you imposed on me?" "To be sure, I do," was his reply. "Well, you can't do it after you accepted my services for Charleston," and I demanded a court-martial before I would finish it. Afterwards Sergeant Hines came from headquarters, saying, "Howell said, Ike got me," "I have no right to inflict a continuance of punishment after accepting his services in some other direction, but confound him, I'll get even with him." Thus matters stood, when some fine day the ball and chain was missing, no one knew what became of it, but somewhere in the middle of the Ogeechee River some two hundred yards below Camp Arnold, it may be found now, having rested there these forty six years.

On the eighth of May we were ordered to Mississippi. We went by the way of Columbus, Ga., arriving there about three o'clock P. M. The ladies had prepared a fine spread for us at the depot. The men were hungry. Capt. F. G. Wilkins being mayor of the City, Mayor Wilkins was Captain of the Columbus Guards, Company B, First Regiment, Georgia Volunteers, and on his return home, after his severe experience of one year's military service, he preferred civil service as more congenial to his feelings. He was a brave and fearless soldier. At Carricks Ford, he and twelve of his men got mixed in with the Yankees, who at that time wore also grey uniforms. They were Ohio troops. Captain Wilkins on seeing his dilemma, formed his men into line, then into column making them go through evolutions, and manual of arms, and marched them to the rear, and out of the Yankee columns without being suspicioned or receiving a scratch. Such coolness is not often exhibited on a danger line, and Captain Wilkins reached Monterey long before any of the Regiment did, and saved himself and his men a great deal of hardship.

When alighting from the train and seeing all those good things prepared for us, I at once took my position. A lady remarked, "Help yourself." I took hold of a piece of fowl, and as I was about to take a bite, someone struck me on the arm with such force that the piece of fowl dropped out of my hand, and someone said, "Those things are not for you." It was Mayor Wilkins. He was glad to see me, and said, "I have something better for you, boys. How many of the First Georgia are here? Get them all together and follow me." We were about a dozen of the old Washington Rifles. He conducted us to a room where we met a committee of gentlemen. After the usual shaking hands and introductions, we passed into another chamber. I never beheld a more bountiful and artistically prepared spread. Provisions arranged on a revolving table, shelved to a pyramid, and loaded with delicious wines. In a corner of the room was a table covered with case liquors of every description, and some fine cigars. I was astonished, I had no idea such delicacies could have been gotten in the whole Confederacy. We surely did enjoy the hospitality of that Committee. Mayor Wilkins introduced me to a Mr. Rothschild, saying, "I want you to take good care of him, he is a splendid fellow." Turning to me he said, "Hermann, I want you to stay all night with this gentleman, he will treat you all right." I said, "Captain Wilkins, I can't leave camps without a permit, and myself and Captain Howell are not on such terms as for me to ask him for any favors." "Well, I'll arrange that, you come along." Captain Wilkins said to Howell, "I want Ike to go home with my friend here," designating Mr. Rothschild. Captain Howell said, "You'll have to be here by seven o'clock, A. M. The train will leave at that time." Mr. Rothschild spoke up, saying, "I'll have him here on time." I was royally treated; the lady of the house and daughter played on the piano and sang. I joined in the chorus 'till late in the night, when I was shown to my room, nicely furnished, a nice clean feather bed and all the requisites for comfort, but I could not sleep, I did not lay comfortable. The two years service I had seen, made a feather bed rather an impediment to my repose, having become accustomed to sleep out doors on the hard ground, with my knapsack as a pillow, so I got up, put my knap sack under my head and lay by the side of the bed on the carpet, and slept like a log the balance of the night; so soundly, that I did not hear the negro boy who was sent to my room to blacken my boots, open the door, but I heard a noise like someone slamming the door and I heard someone running down stairs. I heard many voices talking, and someone coming up stairs, opening the door very unceremoniously, I looked—there was Mr. Rothschild,- greatly astonished and laughing, he could hardly talk. Finally he said, "What in the world made you lay on the floor." I explained to him that being no longer used to sleeping on a bed, I could not rest until I got on the hard floor. Then he told me he had sent up a boy to blacken my boots, who had scared them all by telling them that the man up stairs had fallen off of the bed and lay dead on the floor. I took my ablution, and went down to breakfast, all enjoying that I was still able to do justice to the meal that my kind host and hostess set before me. After many thanks and good byes to Mr. and Mrs. Rothschild and the family, Mr. Rothschild and myself went down to the train, which was in waiting. Everything was soon ready and we departed for Mobile, Ala. At Greenville, Ala., I met General W. H. T. Walker for the first time. Martin's battery was assigned to his brigade. Captain Martin was promoted to Major, and Chief of Staff of General Walker's brigade, and Lieutenant Evan P. Howell, by right of seniority, took his place as Captain. From Mobile, we went to Jackson, Miss.. one section of two cannons were left behind under charge of Lieutenant Robson. The balance arrived at destination at about three o'clock P. M., May 12th, 1863. We unloaded the pieces at once, and all the accoutrements, all the horses and harnessed them up without the loss of any time, took up the line of march towards Raymond Springs. The weather was very warm and the road of red clay was very dusty for men marching in columns. The dust would rise like clouds of ashes at every step. It must be remembered that it was ration day, but we had no time to draw any. As we advanced, we met General Gists' Brigade just out of a fight with General Grant's forces, who landed at Port Gibson, on his forward move to Vicksburg. General Gist had several prisoners. Among them was a Captain. I spoke to him and asked him about the strength of Grant's army. Of course, I did not expect a truthful answer. He replied, "If you'll keep on in the direction you are going, you will meet him. He is not so very far, ahead of you, and when you do meet him, you will think he has more than enough to eat you all up." Well, he did tell the truth, and it has been our misfortune all through the war to fight against many odds. We kept advancing, when of a sudden the command was ordered to halt. We formed ourselves into battery, and I was placed in charge of a detachment. General Walker ordered me to follow him. About two hundred yards ahead the road took a sudden turn around the bluff, which commanded a straight stretch of about a mile. General Walker ordered me to unlimber my gun and place it in position, so as to command that road, and ordered me to fire into any cavalry that might appear. At the further end of my view was a water mill. I remarked, "General, had I not better let them advance somewhat, so as not to waste too much ammunition?" "You must use your own judgment," said he. Looking about me, I saw no infantry in close proximity, so I ventured to ask him where my support was. He answered, "Support Hell!—If they charge you, fight them with the hand spikes, don't you never leave this post," and left.

Mr. James F. Brooks acted as my No. 1. I asked him if he had made his will, if not, he had better, as we were there to stay. We watched with all our eyes, we saw no enemies. Just about dark, we were ordered to limber up, and double quick to the rear, for about a mile, the enemy having taken another route and we were in danger of being cut off. Weary and footsore, having marched about ten miles that afternoon, we retraced our steps within about three miles of Jackson, hungry and thirsty, we marched on, large oaks bordered the road at places and the roots protruded above the surface of the ground; having on a pair of shoes, left foot number six for a number 8 foot, while my right shoe was a number 10 brogan, I crammed cotton in shoe number 10 to prevent too much friction and cut off the end of number 6 to avoid the painful sensation of being cramped, but misfortunes never come single—the night became dark and it threatened to rain. I stumbled over one of those protruding roots and tore off half of my unprotected toe nail on my left foot, a most excruciating and painful sensation. I did not swear, because I was speechless. I mounted the caisson, our horses were jaded, had had no food nor water that day, but managed to get into camp. Dr. Stewart, our surgeon was left at Jackson, with a few of our command who were sick. W. J. Bell was our ambulance driver. He drove me to Dr. Stewart's camp to dress my wound that night. I was all O. K. next morning, when the ball opened after day break. Our pickets announced the enemy's advance. The skirmishes then came into play and kept the advance at some bay for some time, our forces placing themselves in position to receive them in due form. We were five thousand strong, while the enemy numbered twenty-five thousand. At about eleven A. M. orders came from our right to left to fall back, and we gradually withdrew, putting on our prolongs, and firing occasionally as we retraced our steps. When the fight first opened I was in the rear, as stated, on account of my foot, but after being dressed and hearing the firing, I made for the front, and reported to Captain Howell for duty, while he was in line of battle on the extreme left. He said his detachment was complete, to report to the next. Having only four pieces of artillery in action, two under charge of Lieutenant Robson not having yet arrived, they were placed along the front about two hundred yards apart, all had full working force. I retraced my steps and so reported to the Captain, saying, "Well, Captain, there being no use for me here, I shall go to the rear to protect myself and watch the progress of the fight, should there be any casualties in the Company I'll take their place—no use for me to be here unless I can be of some service." Up to that time the skirmish line was still contending for every inch of the ground. Captain Howell says to me, "You stay here, and act as my orderly. I'm hoarse anyhow, and you have a good voice and can repeat my orders and commands," so I was installed by the side of the Captain. The ground on which we stood was a gradual incline, while that of the enemy was about on a level with us, leaving a sort of a basin or valley between both lines. It was a novel sight to see our skirmishers contending every inch of the ground before an overwhelming force, to see them load and fire, and gradually falling back, facing the advancing foe. When suddenly they emerged from the woods, where they were concealed, and advanced in platoon form, sending their deadly missiles into our thin skirmishers ranks. I said, "This is more than our men can stand, let me throw a shell over their heads, into their ranks." He answered, "Do so, but don't shoot our men." "No danger," said I. I depressed the bridge of my piece, raising the muzzle about four fingers. No. four pulled the laniard. It had a good effect, and resulted in stopping their advance, and thus enables our skirmishers to come in. My fire also gave them our position and distance. They at once formed a battery in front of us. I aimed a second shot at a white horse. Captain Howell watching its effect. I being behind the gun, the smoke prevented me from so doing, when he said, "You got him." I soon found out that I had done some damage and that my range was accurate, for they centered their fire of several pieces against my own. One of their shots passed over my gun and knocked off its sight, passed between the detachment, striking the caisson lid in the rear and staving it in, and thus preventing us for a few minutes in replying. We had to break it open with the hand spikes to get ammunition. They undoubtedly thought that we were irreparably silenced, and paid their respects to some other part of our line, but we resumed business again, and they came back at us. I saw a ball rolling on the ground, about six feet to my right. It seemed to be about the same caliber as ours. It rolled up a stump, bouncing about fifteen feet in the air. I thought it was a solid shot and wanting to send it back to them through the muzzle of our gun, I ran after it. It proved to be a shell, as it exploded, and a piece of it struck my arm. It was a painful wound, but not serious. Another ball struck a tree about eight inches in diameter, knocked out a chip, which struck my face and caused me to see the seven stars in plain day light and very near got a scalp of Captain Howell, who stood behind that tree. Orders came for Captain Howell to fall back. He asked me to inform Major Martin, who was in command of the piece at the extreme right, that he was falling back. I had to traverse the whole front of our line. I took the color bearers' horse, a fine animal. We named him Stonewall. The enemy's fire was rather high, as they came up the incline and the balls rattled through the tree tops like hail. It commenced raining very hard. I dismounted and took it afoot. On my way passing the third section, Sim Bland, who acted as number 6, and whose duty it was to carry the ammunition from the caisson and to hand it to No. 2 who inserts it in the muzzle of the gun, while No. 1 rammed it home. As I crossed him at a trot, I remarked, "Sim, this is hot time."

Before he could reply, a solid cannon ball had struck him. Poor fellow, he did not know what hit him, for he was dead. His whole left side entirely torn to pieces.

The enemy was now advancing more rapidly, as our whole line had given away. On my return I found my horse also shot down. I was trying to save the body of Bland, but couldn't get the assistance needed. I went through his pockets and took what he had therein and gave it to his brother, Lieutenant Bland. The enemy pushed me so close I had to take to the woods in my immediate rear, the trees of which somewhat protected me from the enemy's fire. About a hundred yards further I found Sergeant Newsome with his gun and a detachment, trying to make for the public road leading to Jackson. He had managed so far to drive his comman, evading the trees of the forest, when suddenly he was confronted by a plank fence which stood perfectly erect, not a plank missing and about five feet high. He ordered the horses cut out of the harness, and was about to abandon his guns, when I hollered, "No Sergeant, don't do it! Ride through between the posts, they are wide enough apart, knock down the planks." I put myself in action and kicked against the planks, when the whole panel fell over, carrying several others with it, for all the posts were completely rotten at the ground, and thus I saved this piece of artillery and probably the men. We reached the road and marched in column. It was raining hard and every man was soaked to the skin. The column halted, having fallen back about a half a mile, firing as they went, when again we formed in line of battle. I was very tired, and sat down by the road side. When called again into action, I found that I could not use my arm, and that the leaders of my leg had contracted at my groins. The enemy had again out-flanked us, and the men lifted me on a caisson.

The horses stalled. The road being very muddy, the men had to assist at the wheel to pull the carriages out of the mud, by using all their efforts, so I had to get down, for I felt that after all the gun would have to be abandoned, and I did not care to be taken prisoner, but General Joseph E. Johnston made a stand a little further on, until the Yankees outflanked him again. Major Martin happened to be just passing me on his horse. I begged him to take me behind him, as I could not walk. He answered, "It is impossible, we are going to make

another stand. Get in the ambulance." When
the ambulance came in sight, it was full to overflow with wounded and dying. The Major again
rode up. I said "Major Martin, can't you get
me out of my difficulty," he replied, "Hermann,
do the best you can to take care of yourself. If
they capture you, I will have you exchanged as
soon as possible." Poor consolation, I thought,
but I was determined not to be taken if I possibly could help it, so I started towards Jackson,
taking the edge of the woods, first on account of
the mud, then as somewhat of a protection from
the bullets. My locomotion was slow, from eight
to ten inches was the longest strides I was able
to make, and this with excruciating pains. Presently our forces rushed past me and formed
again into line of battle, thus leaving me between both lines, the bullets coming from either
direction, when again I entered our line. This
maneuvre happened three times before I reached
Jackson, in a stretch of three miles. It was
then four o'clock p. m.

CHAPTER XII.

When we reached Jackson the previous day I noted a flat by the side of the railroad bridge. I was thinking to cross Pearl River by that means, so I started to the right towards the railroad bridge. On my way down the street a lady was standing over a tub of whiskey with a dipper in her hand. She said to me, "Poor fellow, are you wounded?" I said, "Yes." She dipped up a dipper full of whiskey, which I drank. It had a good effect on my shattered nerves and did not cause me the least dizziness. It was the medicine I surely needed. On arriving at the River, I found the flat was gone, the railroad bridge was the only chance left me to cross. I crawled up the embankment and found that the cross ties were too far apart for me to step it, owing to my contracted leaders, so I concluded to "coon it" on my hands and knees on the stringers, holding onto the rail.

The bridge is a long one and very high, Jackson being built on a high bluff. When about half way across I heard a great deal of noise and reports of fire arms; I heard bullets whizzing by. Finally bullets were hitting the trestle beneath me and in front of me. Looking back I saw at a distance of about four hundred yards a force of the enemy, which I judged to be about half a regiment, coming up the lowlands in a flank around Jackson. My first impulse was, can I make it across, or must I surrender? I concluded to take the chances, and continued to cross. Bullets were striking beneath me, and in front, splinters were flying. One ball hit the rail about six inches in front of my hand. They were gaining on me fast, when at last I reached the other side, laying myself flat on the track, I rolled over, down about an eighteen foot embankment. Thus being protected from the enemy's bullets, I entered the swamp not far beside the road leading to Branton, I noted a large hollow poplar tree. It must have been four or five feet in diameter. I crawled in, I felt faint and weak, had not eaten anything that day. I must have fainted; when presently I heard the sound of artillery and musketry to my right across the river and the noise of an empty wagon coming from towards Branton. I took a reconnoitering look, and saw Jackson on fire and a wagon driven by a negro, holding the lines over four splendid mules, coming towards the city. I took my stand in the road, pistol in hand. The following conversation ensued:

"Halt. Where are you going?"

"To Jackson. Marse Richard sent me to fotch his things. He is afraid the Yankees would cotch him."

"How will you get across?"

"Goes on the flat, sah."

"There is no flat now."

"Yes there is, and Marse Richard——"

"Turn the head of the mules towards Branton, or you are a dead Negro"—aiming at him as I spoke. He exclaimed, "Don't shoot Marster, I'll do as you say." He turned the mules towards where he came from. I crawled behind in the wagon, pistol in hand, and at a gallop all the way for twelve miles. We entered Branton in the early part of the night. The people were still up at the Hotel. The excitement ran high about the enemies capturing Jackson. Branton was a nice little village. The negro proved to be a run-away. Had stolen the team from the quarter-master and running with it to the enemy. The lady of the hotel came to me saying, "Are you wounded?" I stated my condition, and she sympathized with me, saying, "Poor fellow, I expect you need something to eat." I surely did, for I was more dead than alive, after having passed such an eventful day. I ate a hearty supper. I was given a shirt. She bandaged my arm, which was smarting badly. She furnished me a room and a bottle of mustang linament to rub myself. My clothes which were full of mud were washed and dried by a large fire. The following morning, I felt really refreshed. It is unnecessary to say that I slept well that night. At an early hour that morning, the alarm of "The Yankees are coming. They are only four miles from here and Johnston is retreating towards Canton." Everybody that could get away, left. The quartermaster had an old broken down horse, which he tendered me for having saved his fine team, and I left the town on horse back, thanking my hostess for all her kindness. About two miles from Branton I met up with three men from my Company, viz, A. P. Heath, Jackson O'Quinn and Harmon Fields. They were not in the fight, having been on the sick list and not fit for duty, so we traveled together for some distance. We reached a settlement, which from appearance, belonged to well-to-do people. The gentleman of the premises was standing at the gate leading to the house. I said to my comrades that I would have to rest and recuperate until I got well, so I addressed myself to the proprietor, "Sir, can you take care of a wounded Confederate? He put his hand in his hip pocket in quick motion, as if to draw a pistol, but instead drew a small slate and pencil, handed it to me with a motion to write my request, which I did. He rubbed it out and wrote swiftly in a scholarly style, "Nothing I have is too good for a Confederate soldier. Walk in—all of you." His name was Williams, unfortunately deaf and dumb, but very intelligent. His family consisted of a wife and two daughters, and all seemed to be well educated and comfortably situated. They were very solicitous in their attentions to us. The girls played on the piano while I entertained the old man, by writing on his slate my experience of the previous day. He looked at me in wonder, and occasionally took hold of my hand and shook it. I remained his guest for nearly a week, until we located our Company, and where to meet it. I got entirely well, my arm was healing nicely, under the care of Mrs. Williams. Our forces had located at Canton. He sent us mule-back through Pearl River Swamp to the Canton road, while I rode my horse. He refused to take any remuneration for anything he had done for us, so I sent back my horse with a note and begged him to accept the same and thanking them all for what they had done for us.

CHAPTER XIII.

The following day I entered camp with my comrades among great cheers, all having thought me dead or a prisoner. Major Martin asked me how I got through. I told him I took his advice and did the best I could. I related to him the incidents that I met with. He said, "Well, I congratulate you. I don't believe one in a thousand would have escaped." "I was glad I was the one." We were ordered to strike tents at Canton, and we retraced our steps again towards Jackson, a distance of between twenty and twenty-five miles. It was one of the hottest days of the season. The road bed being red clay. Our forces now amounted to about eight thousand men, and marching in column with artillery, wagon train and all the paraphernalia appertaining to a moving army, raised such intense dust that it was impossible to recognize one's file-leader in his immediate front. Every step of every individual raised clouds of dust, which lay ankle deep. It was actually suffocating. Men and horses would gasp for breath. The men occasionally would expectorate large lumps of clay that settled in their throats, and no water to be had. We didn't pass a single stream of any kind. It was a forced march to get in the enemy's rear and to cut off re-inforcement and supplies for Grant's invading forces onto Vicksburg. The enemy was also making back to Jackson on the Clinton Road which ran nearly parallel to the Canton Road, and we could see their advance by the column of dust to our right. Just before dark a very heavy rain and thunder storm set in. It was preferable to the previous conditions of the weather, although it put us half leg deep in sticky red mud. It got so dark we could not see anything and the rain continued pouring down in all its fury. It was nip and tuck as to which army would reach Jackson first. We got there just a little ahead of the enemy in time to occupy the ditches which now were nearly knee deep in water. In that condition we passed the night, expecting to be attacked momentarily. Men were detailed long in the rear to cook rations for the men in the ditch, which were issued along the line, and consisted of corn bread cooked (a la hate) and a piece of fat bacon. A very amusing incident happened to one of my comrades, W. A. Grimes, who early on our march, and before the dust got so dense, had to step aside for some reason, and being detained while the column kept onward, threw him some distance behind his command. The State of Georgia had sent her troops some shoes; the description of my draw I have already stated, and some white wool hats. Grimes put his name on the front of his hat in large capital letters, and as he hurried to catch up with his command, someone hollowed as he passed, "How are you Bill Grimes?" Grimes stopped in surprise to see who knew him in some other command. Others took up the word all along the line of "How are you Bill Grimes?" Grimes hurried on, on his way, the perspiration running down his face, which had the appearance of being covered with a mask. He could not account for his sudden popularity until he pulled off his hat to wipe off his face. He saw his name on his hat and quickly turned it wrong side out. His name had passed all along the column faster than he could travel and passed Howell's Battery long before he caught up with it. Early in the morning the enemy made demonstrations all along our line and was repulsed. It had quit raining. The artillery kept up a desultory fire for eight days and nights. The enemy's forces were at least three to our one and therefore, could relieve each other, while we were obliged to be kept continually on duty, and consequently became exhausted, my eyes were blood shot, men loaded and fired mechanically, and when so exhausted that I couldn't stand any longer, I dropped beside one of the pieces and in a jiffy, was asleep. I couldn't even hear the report of the guns within a few feet of me. The strain was more than my physique could stand. I got sick and unconscious, and when I came to myself, I was in Yazoo City in a private house, snugly fixed, and a kindly lady by my bedside, whose name was Mrs. Lyons. She cried for joy to see me recover my senses. I asked her where I was and how long I had been there. She said just a week. I asked her what place it was and she said "Yazoo City." I shall always remember gratefully the kind treatment I received from that worthy family, and when after a week's convalescence, I took my leave with many thanks. The lady said she hoped that her brother who was in the Virginia army would in case of sickness receive the attention that she would bestow on any Confederate soldier. Such was the spirit that prevailed throughout the Confederate States.

CHAPTER XIV.

I rejoined my command at Morton station on the M. & O. Railroad. The object of the second fight at Jackson, as I understood it, was to get in the rear of the investing army of Vicksburg under General Grant. General Joseph E. Johnston expected a reinforcement, sufficient so as to cut off supplies from the invading army, and to attack it in the rear, while General Pemberton might make a sortie and attack it in the front, and thus save Vicksburg from capture. Our reinforcement never came. We then moved to Vaughn Station and thus hung in the rear of Grant, but not strong enough to venture an attack, unless in concert with General Pemperton who was defeated at Big Black and bottled up in Vicksburg, his stronghold. A very sad incident happened in our camp. Lieutenant Ruben Bland, a very kind officer and beloved by all his men, died. His brother Sim, as stated, was killed at the first fight at Jackson. They were very much attached to each other and brooding over his misfortune, some thought he took opium with suicidal intent, others thought otherwise. The writer was sitting on a box on the railroad platform, smoking his pipe. Close to the platform stood the Company's ambulance. In passing me Lieutenant Bland remarked, "Well, Ike, you seem to enjoy your pipe," I answered, "I do, I smoke the pipe of peace," he smiled and said, "Yes, everything looks peaceable here, I believe I am going to take a nap in this ambulance." About a quarter of an hour after, Quinten Dudley who was Hospital Steward, had cause to get some medicine out of the medicine chest that Dr. Stewart kept in the ambulance. He immediately gave the alarm that Lieutenant Bland was dead. I could not believe it. I jumped off the platform into the ambulance, and there lay Lieutenant Bland stretched out in full length, his face purple. Dr. Stewart, who at once was on hand opened an artery on top of his head. He bled freely. He tried to get up artificial respiration by working his arm back and forth, but to no avail. Bland was dead beyond recovery and mourned by every member of the Company.

It was on a very warm June day when I concluded to have a general cleaning up. It must be remembered that we lost all of our personal effects, which we destroyed to keep them from falling into the enemy's hands, and our wardrobes only consisted of what we carried on our backs and filth begot what we called "creepers", and one not used to such made him feel most miserable, so I took a camp kettle which also served for our culinary purposes to boil my clothes in, and while they were drying in the sun, I crept into the bushes in the shade and fell asleep. During my repose some miscreant stole my shirt, and for several weeks I did not have a shirt on my back, so one day it came to my knowledge that Gen. W. H. T. Walker, our Division Commander, having been promoted, and Colonel Claude Wilson, was appointed as Brigadier General in his place, offered a reward of thirty days furlough and a fine saddle horse to ride during the war to any man that would carry a dispatch to General Pemperton who was then besieged in Vicksburg. I told Sergeant Hines if any man needed a furlough I did, in the fix I was in. I believe I will go and offer my services. He laughed and said, "Well, good luck old fellow." So I started to headquarters which were in an abandoned farm house, about a quarter of a mile distant from where our battery was in camp. I walked to the sentinel who halted me. I want to see Gen. Walker. "You can't get in." "Call the officer of the guard," says I, which he did and the Lieutenant came up. I stated to him that I wanted to see Gen. Walker. "Follow me," says he, which I did. There were at least from twenty to twenty-five officers of all grades sitting in a large room, engaged, it seemed to me, in social conversation. I walked straight up to General Walker and stated my business, and what I had heard he offered to any man who would successfully carry a dispatch to General Pemperton at Vicksburg. "I thought, if any man needed a furlough, it was I." Opening my jacket which was closely buttoned, although it was à hot day in July, I displayed my nakedness. "I have not even, as you see, a shirt to wear." It raised a giggle among some of the officers, while others looked upon me in sympathy. I stated how I lost that only shirt I possessed. Just at that time entered Major Martin. Recognizing me, he said, "Hermann, you here?" He seemed rather surprised. I stated the object of my visit. He turned to General Walker, saying, "General, I stand sponsor for this man. He belongs to my battery, and he is one of the best." I inclined my head in recognition of the compliment paid me, and he extended me his hand. In the meantime, General Walker called me and said, "You see that small trunk in yonder corner. Therein is my wardrobe. I believe I have three shirts therein; that is all I have—I divide —go and get you one. We are about the same size. I hope it will fit you." I made for the little hairy trunk, no bigger than a good hand valise and slightly oval, opened the lid, saying, "Beggars ought not to be choosers. I will take the first I come to," which was a clean white shirt, with cuffs and collars attached. Off went my jacket in the presence of the company; into the garment I went, feeling a thousand per cent. better. I said, "Well, General, I've heard of some stepping into other men's shoes, but never before have I known of a high private slipping into a General's shirt at one jump." This brought a big laugh from the assembly, the General joining heartily. I thanked him and extended my hand in token of my appreciation. He remarked, "You are surely welcome, come around tomorrow at eleven o'clock A. M., and we will talk matters over." He asked, "Have you ever been to Vicksburg." "No Sir." "Do you know anything about the country around, and about the City?" "This is my first experience in these diggins." "How would you manage?" "I'll be governed by circumstances as they present themselves." After a pause he repeated, "Come around tomorrow at eleven o'clock." I gave the military salute and started towards the door, when he called me saying, "Do you ever drink anything?" I answered, "General, this is a strange question. Why didn't Jack eat his supper? I've not seen a drop since we left Jackson," and I stated how I got that. He laughed and said, "Go in that room," indicating the door with his index finger. "You will find a table in there with liquors, I think a good drink will do you good." One invitation was sufficient. I stepped into the next room, and there I beheld a round table loaded with all kinds of bottles, containing different liquors, some labeled different kinds of whiskies, brandies, gin, schedam, schnapps, etc. I took the square bottle of schedam and poured me out a stiff drink, thanked the General and departed for my camp, but not being in the habit of drinking, I felt the effects of the liquor. I felt somewhat, what I may call buoyant, and in for any fun. I met Sergeant W. H. Hines. He said, "Ike, what luck?" "The best in the world," tapping myself on the breast. "You see that shirt, this once was General Walker's, now it's mine." I told him all that passed at headquarters. The next day I reported as directed. The General said, "Well, Hermann, the jig is up. While we were talking about the matter yesterday, Pemberton surrendered, and

WAR BETWEEN THE STATES 125

I therefore do not need your services." I said, well, I wish he had held out until some other day than the fourth of July." The General said, "Yes."

As I started to camp, the General said, "Well, Hermann I thank you anyhow for your offer and you shall have a furlough all the same. I give you two weeks. I hope you will have a nice time." Major Martin who was present said also, he hoped I would have a nice time. I replied, "Major, I have not a cent of money, how can I have a nice time. We have not been paid off since we left Savannah. Have you some money? If so I would like to borrow until I get mine from the Government." He said, he had a fifty dollar bill. If it would do me any good, 1 could have it. He handed me the bill which was then worth about two or three dollars in specie. Such was the depreciation of our currency. I went into the interior about ten miles from camp. The people were downcast. They did not know what would become of them. Jackson, the capital of the State, in the hands of the enemy. Vicksburg, a large and well fortified city and defended by a large army had surrendered and its defenders taken prisoners. The people were in despair, not knowing what evil awaited them. I soon found out that camps among the boys was the more congenial place for me, so after an absence of three days I returned.

CHAPTER XV.

So one good afternoon, J. B. Thomas, a good clever comrade and good soldier, and myself took a stroll and incidentally looking for something to eat. We passed a vegetable garden, a luxury we seldom enjoyed. On the side of the pailings were some squashes. Thomas remarked, I wish I had some of them. I said, "Well, slip one of those palings and get a few, I'll be on the watch out." No sooner said than done. Thomas gathered about a dozen the size of my fist. He stuck them in his shirt bosom. I gave him the alarm that the lady was watching him. As he looked up he saw her at the other end of the garden. He started through the opening he had made quicker than a rabbit could have done when pursued by hounds. Thomas is a man of small statue and very short legged, but he split the air to beat the band. We were both in our shirt sleeves, no vests, only wore pants confined around the waist by a belt, the squashes were bobbing up and down in his shirt, as he progressed and the proprietress after him. Finally the squashes lifted the shirt out of his confines and down came the squashes rolling on the ground. Thomas did not stop, but casting a regretful side glance at his booty, he sped on to camp, while his garment was floating to the breeze, caused by his velocity. When the woman reached the spot where the squashes lay scattered,, she stopped, looking after the fleeing individual and sending a full vocabulary of invectives after him. I who had followed leisurely caught up while she gathered her squashes into her apron. I remarked, "Madam, you seem to have spilled your vegetables." "No, it was not me that spilled them, it's that good for nothing somebody, there he runs—he stole them out of my garden." I said, "He ought not to have done it, if I knew who he was I would report him." She said, "I would not have minded to give him some if he had asked me for them, but I don't like for anybody to go into my garden and take what belongs to me." Poor woman, she had no idea that within a few days after our departure, the enemy would appear and not only appropriate the needful, but would destroy all the rest to keep her from enjoying any of it. She offered me some of the squashes which I accepted with thanks. I carried them to Thomas, saying she would have given you some if you had asked for them. Thomas replied, he wished he had known it.

CHAPTER XVI.

The fall of Vicksburg ended the Mississippi Campaign, and our troops were ordered to join the Army of Tennessee. All had left with the exception of the Mississippi Regiment and our battery who were awaiting transportation. Our commissary had also gone ahead of us and so we were left to "root hog or die." We had to eat once in awhile any how. Quinton Dudley and myself took a stroll to the commissary of the Mississippi Regiment. I learned that his name was Coleman. Passing through the building which was an old wooden railroad warehouse about a hundred feet long and forty wide, Quinton picked up a piece of rock salt from a large pile. Captain Coleman saw him put something in his haversack. In a brisk manner, said, "What is that you have taken?" He showed him a piece of salt the size of a hen egg. "Put it back," he hollowed at him. Quinton threw it back on the pile very much humiliated. On our leaving the building, I spied on the platform at the other end of the warehouse a large hogshead full of smoked meat of all descriptions, there were sides, shoulders and hams. They looked very enticing for hungry men like we were. We went to camp and reported how that Captain had caught Quinton who was very timid and did not like to be caught in the act. Others felt different about such. We were entitled to a living while in the field on duty. Some suggested that we go and charge the commissary and get some rations. I said, "That would bring on some trouble. Maybe we might get some of that meat by strategy," so we planned that W. N. Harmon should take ten men around and about the warehouse, while I would engage the Captain in conversation, during which time Harmon and his men would help themselves to rations. I awaited an opportune moment when Captain Coleman was at the other end of the building from where the hogshead of meat stood. Entering by that end, I walked squarely up to the Captain, extending my hand. "How do you do, Captain Coleman? I'm very glad to meet you, it is an unexpected pleasure. How long since you have heard from home?" He looked at me in surprise, holding onto my hand. I heard some meat drop on the ground. I knew the meat was flying campwards. "Well," said Capt. Coleman, "you have the advantage of me.' "Don't you know me?" says I? He replied, "Well, your face is familiar to me, but I can't place you. Are you not from Emanuel county,

"Madam, have you spilled your vegetables?"
I enquired

Georgia?" "No, but I have some kinfolks in Georgia with my name." "Well, then I am mistaken and beg your pardon." "We have a lake on the Ogeechee River called Coleman's Lake. I went there often for fishing, and was sure you were one of the Colemans that lived there when at home. You favor them very much." "Well, said he, they may be some kin to me." By that time, between thirty and forty pieces of meat had changed hands. The next morning transportation came, and we loaded the cars which carried us to the Tennessee Army, then under the command of General Bragg, who was then retreating, leaving Tennessee to the tender care of the Federals, under command of General Rosencrantz. Our forces took a stand around and about Lookout Mountain and Chickamauga. We struck camp some distance from the main forces after unloading the train and watering and feeding the horses. The boys took a swim in the river, a luxury not realized for many days past. I was detailed to cut underbrush in the woods to assist stretching ropes to corral our horses. I was not quite as green in handling an axe by this time as I was in Virginia, when I was detailed to cut wood for the blacksmith shop. I was again taken sick with risings in my ear. I suffered as only those who ever suffered with such affliction knew how to extend their sympathy. The pains were simply excruciating and threw me into hot fever. We were ordered to strike camps. We marched that forenoon until eleven o'clock. The sun was shining in full force. I could no longer keep up. I stopped by the roadside and lay down, waiting for the Company's baggage wagon to come along. Lorenzo Stephens was the driver. After awhile he appeared on foot. One of the rear axles of his wagon having broken, he therefore hurried forward to get some assistance. In the meantime, the ambulance came along in charge of the Company surgeon. He had me picked up and placed in it. He said I had high fever and gave me some medicine, and as we passed the station of a railroad, the name of which I did not know, I was put on the train with others and sent to the Atlanta Hospital, in charge of Dr. Paul Eve, of Augusta, Dr. Rosser being in charge of my ward. I was suffering terribly, both of my ears were discharging corruption. Through suffering and hardship, my general health was giving away. I needed rest and time to recuperate. Medicines were hard to get, and I was slow in recovering my strength. One day Dr. Rosser asked me if I would like to have a furlough. He thought it would help me. I said, "Yes, the best in the world, as soon as I can gain a little strength," so he and Dr. Eve came to my cot the following morning, and after examining my condition, departed. Dr. Rosser came again in the afternoon and handed me a thirty days furlough. I was very grateful to him. He was a perfect gentleman, hard working and sympathetic. I came home to my foster mother, Mrs. Jas. L. Braswell, under whose care I soon gained strength.

CHAPTER XVII.

Before leaving the hospital I requested Dr. Rosser to inform my Captain of my whereabouts and of my physical condition, which he promised he would do, and I have no doubts he did. While at home I also corresponded with some of my comrades. I enjoyed my furlough at Fenns Bridge among my friends. Colonel Sol. Newsome, Hudson W. Sheppard, Bennett Hall, W. J. Lyons, Daniel Inman and others, who came after their mail and incidentally brought their fishing tackle and guns to fish and hunt in the Ogeechee river and swamp. In the meantime discussing the ups and downs of the men in the field. The above named citizens were all slave owners and above the requisite age for military duty. It was quite a pastime for me to hear them discuss among themselves the politics of that day, for be it understood they were not exactly a unit in sentiment as regards secession. They were about equally divided; some for the union, while those who differed brought some of the most convincing arguments to my mind to bear on the situation, and although young in the cause of politics, I was obliged to take sides with them, as a matter of right, as we saw it. Those who opposed did not question our right, but differed as to the policy pursued. They contended that we were wrong in judgment as the sequel had proven. In fact, we were not prepared for such tremendous onslaughts as we had to meet, and we believed and had reliance on our so-called friends across Mason and Dixon line, which proved to be as bitter as the rankest abolitionists. One morning, Mr. Brantley came up and brought the Georgian, a county news paper, saying, "Hermann, your name is in this paper." I said, "Is it?" "Listen."

"The following men are absent from their Commands without leave, and should they not immediately report for duty, they will be reported as deserters: J. J. Sheppard, I. Hermann and others whose names I have forgotten. It was signed Captain Evan P. Howell, commanding battery. I said, "Gentlemen, it is a lie, and here is the proof, showing my sick furlough from Dr. Paul Eve." Mr. Lyons then spoke up, "Well, what are you going to do about it?" I walked into cousin Abe's store, took a sheet of paper and addressed, Mr. J. N. G. Metlock, Editor of the Sandersville Georgian,"

"My dear sir:—

In perusing your previous issue I noted Capt. Evan P. Howell's advertisement, which among others I was named as one absent without leave, and should I not report immediately to my command, he would publish me as a deserter. Now in simple justice to myself, I wish to inform Capt. Howell, as well as the public, that his statement is false, that I have a furlough granting me leave of absence and that under no consideration would I be away from my command,

Very respectfully,

I. Hermann.

At Home.

P. S.—Please forward copy of your next issue to Captain Howell and charge expenses to me."

I returned to my friends and said, "Gentlemen, this is my reply, and when my time is up, I shall report, either to Dr. Paul Eve, or Captain Howell." Colonel Sol Newsome tapped me on the shoulder, saying, "Hurrah, Hurrah for you, Hermann." In a few days later, Sergeant W. H. Hines, and four men of my Company came to arrest me. I said to them, "You can't do it as long as I have authority to remain here," and showed them my furlough, which lacked about two weeks of having expired. They were all glad I was properly fixed and so expressed themselves. They were also glad of the opportunities they had to call upon their respective families, which they would not have had otherwise.

From Fenns Bridge I went to Macon to spend a few days with a cousin who lived there. As I walked the street one named Colson who belonged to the Provost Guard came up saying, "Ike old fellow, I have orders to arrest you." "What for, Colson?" He answered, he did not know. "Who gave you the orders?" He said "Major Roland." "Let us go up and see him." We walked up from Cherry Street to Triangular block, where Roland, who was commander of the Post, had his headquarters. The room was full of men and officers, among whom I recognized Captain Napier, who had lost a limb in Virginia; the rest were all strangers to me. Major Roland addressed himself to me "What can I do for you?" "You had me arrested." Colson was standing there; I looked at him; he said "You gave me the orders." "What is your name?" "Isaac Hermann." Roland brightened up; "You are the fellow I was after; you are reported as a deserter." I pulled my furlough, which was somewhat dilapidated from constant wear and tear; he scrutinized it closely, handing it back to me, saying, "This paper is forged; some brother countryman fixed it up for you." "You are a liar," I said. Quick as lightning he grabbed and drew his sword, which was lying on the table, exclaiming as he faced me, "I am an officer." In the meantime I executed a half about, drawing my pistol, saying: "I am a private; if you make a move I'll put daylight through you." And there we stood, facing each other for a few seconds, when one of the officers in the room approached me, saying in a whisper, "Put up your pistol, I am your friend." "Who are you?" "I am Paton Colquitt, Colonel of the 46th Ga. Reg't., stationed at Charleston, S. C., I am on my way to my command, but intend now to remain to see you out." I extended my hand and he shook it heartily. Major Roland looked very pale; the rest of the company present looked on with interest. Roland ordered a Sergeant and four men as a guard to escort me to the guard house. I said "I'll die first, right here, before I'll march through Macon, guarded like a horse thief. I have not done anything to be arrested for; I am known in Macon and will not submit to any such indignity." Colonel Colquitt stepped up to the table, saying, "Will you take me as sponsor for this gentleman, to report at any place you may designate, without a guard?" Roland could not refuse, so trembling he wrote me (a billet de logement): "To the Officer in Command at the Calaboose: Admit the Bearer. By order of Major Roland, Commanding Provost Post, Macon, Georgia." Before calling at the prison I passed to where my cousin lived. I stated what had happened, so that she would not look for me, as I was stopping at her house. She was much distressed and feared personal harm would befall me. I reassured her the best I knew how and requested her to let me have a blanket, if she could spare one, so that I could sleep on it that night. I rolled the blanket, tied the ends together with a string and drew it across my shoulder. On the way I thought of the threat Captain Howell made at Bryant County, Camp Arnold, when Sergt. Hines reported to me what he said, that he would get me yet. I was mad; I was honor bound to report at the calaboose. Col. Colquitt was my sponsor, I could not go back on him. Finally I arrived at the prison, an old building, about 25 by 40; it might have been used as a stable. I presented my ticket for admittance, the officer looked at it, read it, then looked at me and smiled, and said, "Well, this is unusual." I disengaged myself of the blanket, as he unlocked the door. The room was packed with men, among them some Yankees, or some in Federal uniforms. As the door was locked behind me one of the inmates hollowed. "There is a new comer, he must sing us a song;" I remarked, I rather felt like fighting than singing just now, when a big strapping fellow presented himself, with his coat off, saying, as he put himself in a fighting attitude, "Here is your mule;" I answered as I hit him, "Here is your rider." I struck him such an unexpected blow that it stunned him, when he said he had enough, as I was to double him. He apologized, saying he was just funning; I answered and said, "I meant it, and you believe it now; I am obliged to you for having given me this opportunity, for I have been badly treated." I need not say that I was respectfully treated by the rest of the inmates. And while room to lay down was at a premium, I had all I needed for that purpose. The following morning at the break of day, my name was called at the wicket; I answered. The door swung open and there stood Col. Colquitt, smiling. "Well, you are a free man"; "How did you do it?" "Ask me no questions and I'll tell you no lies." I said, "Let me get my blanket I borrowed on the way." He answered: "The train that will carry me to my regiment will leave in half an hour, and I have done what I intended before going; I wish I had a thousand men like you, and I would walk through Yankeedom." I thanked him heartily for what he said and did, promising never to forget it, and I never have. We walked some distance together, the atmosphere was chilly, and I proposed to him if he would accept a treat from me in the way of a drink; he said, "With great pleasure." We found a place on our way to the depot, which was not very far, as the Calaboose was situated a little back of the Brown House, and we drank a drink of as mean potato whiskey, the only kind the men had, at one dollar a dram, that was ever distilled.

CHAPTER XVIII.

As matters now stood, I was determined not to return to my Company until I was entirely recovered to my usual health. So I reported to Dr. Green in charge of the Floyd House Hospital for treatment. He asked me what was the matter with me; I told him I did not know. He stripped me and made a thorough examination, and when he got through he said, "You have an enlargement of the heart, and ought not to be exposed." He prescribed for me, and I reported to him daily until my furlough had expired. I felt a great deal better and was about ready to return to my command, but Dr. Green advised me not to do it yet awhile. I said, "My furlough is out;" He said, "That does not make any difference, you are under my charge for the present." In the meantime Major Roland was removed as Commander of the Post at Macon and Col. Aiken was appointed in his stead. While in the Hospital I made myself useful, and Dr. Green appointed me General Ward-Master. My duties were to look over the entire wards and see that those under me did their duty, and that all inmates were properly attended to. One good morning Sergt. Haywood Ainsworth came to me, saying, "Ike I have in my possession a letter for the Commander of the Post, Col. Aiken, from Capt. Evan P. Howell; he is giving you the devil; he sent me after you. If you go with me to the command I will not deliver it." I said, "Haywood, do you know what he writes in that letter?" "No, not exactly, but it is very severe." "I'd like to see what he says." "Have you seen Col. Aiken; does he know you?" No. "I will tell you what we will do; you give me the letter and I will deliver it myself; you can see that I do it, he will not know me from you, as he does not know either of us." Ainsworth laughed and says, "Well as you say." So we both marched up to the Provost Marshal's office. Col. Aiken was sitting in a chair at his desk. I walked up to him, gave him the military salute, handed him the letter and took my position behind his chair, looking over his shoulder as he read the letter. Capt. Howell did not at all times write a very legible hand for one not used to his writing; hence I being used to it, got through before the Colonel did, I took a little step to my left and rear, awaiting Col. Aiken's orders. "Sergeant, where is the man?" asked he. "He is in the Floyd house hospital, in charge of Dr. Green." "Is he sick." "I suppose so." "Then he is under proper authority, I can do nothing in this case, as it stands. You go and see Dr. Green and ask him if Hermann is well enough to be discharged and go to camp. If so and he refuses to go, come to me and I will give the necessary assistance required." I thanked him, saying, "Col. I do not think there will be any necessity for me to trouble you further," and Haywood and myself left, laughing all the way. Sergt. Ainsworth then said, Well Ike, you are a good one, I know you won't give me away. I said, You surely do not think that of me. Oh no! I have all confidence in you. Well, what are you going to do? I will go back with you; I shall face the gentleman and tell him what I think of him. What was in the letter, what did he say? He stated in the letter that I was a very desperate character; that I left in time of battle; that he had used all his efforts to get me back to my command, and had failed. To please give Sergt. Ainsworth all necessary assistance to accomplish that object. Continuing, I said, Haywood, you like to go home; so do I. Suppose we go to Washington county for a few days, say until Friday. You living in town put a notice in the paper, stating that you will return to our camp which is now at Dalton, and will take pleasure in forwarding anything that may be sent to the boys from their friends and families. Sergt. Ainsworth said, That is a good idea. I said, Well I will meet you at Tennille Friday on the night train. But before we go, I must have the approval of Dr. Green, under whose charge I now am; so we went to see Dr. Green: I stated to him that I would like to return to my command. He said, You are not well enough to do camp duty. I said, Well, under circumstances as they are, I am willing to take my chances. I stated to him the facts as they were, in the presence of Sergt. Ainsworth, who coincided to everything I said. Then I remarked, Doctor, you have been very kind to me, and done me lots of good, for which I am very grateful, but I can't rest under such imputation; I intend to straighten matters out. So he said, Well, if I can do anything for you or be any service to you, let me know what it is and I will be glad to do it. I said, All I want is for you to give me a statement under what condition I placed myself under your care, and the date of my admittance and discharge, and your opinion as to my present condition for active service. He said he would do that, he would make a statement and have it ready in an hour. In the meantime Sergt. Ainsworth and myself took a stroll through the city. I told my relatives and friends good bye. We returned to the hospital, they were all sorry I left them. Doctor Green gave me the papers I required, I put them in my pocket unopened. He said, If there is anything else you need, let me know. I thanked him very kindly, and we left for Washington county. Sergt. Ainsworth said to me, Dr. Green seems to think a great deal of you; he seems to be a perfect gentleman. I said, Yes, everybody who comes in contact with him likes him; he is a very conscientious Doctor and is very attentive to his business. Friday night I took the train at Davisboro; I had about a dozen boxes for the boys in camp, under my charge at Tennille. Sergt. Ainsworth met me with as many more boxes, and we travelled to Dalton; it took us two nights and a day to get there. It was Sunday morning early, when we reached camp. The boys were all glad to see us, we delivered our trust and there was plenty of good things to eat in camp, in consequence of our forethought. During my absence from camp Dr. Stewart was transferred and Dr. Beauchamp took his place. I had never seen him before, so I at once reported to him, gave him my papers from Dr. Green and he at once relieved me from active duty. Then I stated to

"I am a private—if you make a move I'll put daylight through you."

him why I had returned to camp, and the feud that existed between Capt. Howell and myself, and what he had done and said. So I was determined to face the worst. I walked about that day among the boys in camp, all of whom were my friends; if I had an enemy in camp outside of Capt. Howell, I did not know it. About four o'clock p. m. I bethought myself since I was not arrested after the awful charges having been made against me, I had probably better report my presence, although every one in camp, Captain included, knew I was there. So I just met Sergt. Hines, being very intimate with him, I said, Bill, you want to have some fun? Come with me, I am going to report at headquarters; since all that hullabaloo I am still unmolested. The officers quarters were about one hundred yards up on a ridge from where the pieces were parked. Capt. Howell was sitting in front of his tent. I gave him the salute, saying, Well, here I am. He answered, I thought I never would see you again. I said probably you would not, if it had not been for some d——d lies written to Col. Aiken, Provost Marshal at Macon. Who wrote them? Capt. Evan P. Howell, Comdg. Battery. If you think that I am afraid of powder and ball, try me ten steps. Do you mean it as a challenge? You are an officer; I am a private; it is for you to construe it as you see fit. I'll have you courtmartialed and shot. I dare you to do it. In the meantime Sergt. Hines was swinging to my jacket and we withdrew. So Hines said, If I had known that you would get mad that way I would not have come with you. So I remarked, I wanted you to come and be a witness, as to what should pass between him and me. A half hour later Sergt. Hines came to me, saying, Ike, you are on duty tonight. By whose orders? Capt. Howell's. I said, It is not a rule to put a man on guard duty who had passed two nights in succession without sleep, he might fall asleep on his post. However, I did not come here to do duty, I merely came to see what punishment Capt. Howell would inflict on me, as he stated that I deserted; and again, I am relieved from duty by Dr. Beauchamp. Sergt. Hines made his report. I saw Capt. Howell hastily walk over to Dr. Beauchamp's quarters and expostulated with him as to my ability of doing duty, thus impugning the Doctor's capacity as a physician, he who after a thorough examination having passed on my condition; I heard Dr. Beauchamp speaking in a loud voice: "Capt. Howell, if you would attend to your duty as faithfully as I do mine you would get along better with your men.'' Howell replied that he would have me examined by a Board of Physicians. That's all right, that is exactly what Hermann asked me to have done and I have already set him down to meet the Board at Dalton on next Wednesday. In the meantime Dr. Beauchamp treated me and I reported to him daily, when able to be up; if not he came to my quarters.

CHAPTER XIX.

Wednesday came, the day I was to report before the Board; I was not feeling as well as I had a day or so previous. I went to Bell, our ambulance driver, saying Joe, I have to meet the Board today at Dalton, you will have to carry me there. He answered he could not do it as he had orders from Capt. Howell to have the ambulance ready for him, as he wanted to make a social call, so I said no more. Dr. Beauchamp who saw me walking about in camp, came to me saying, I thought you were going to Dalton today. I said I would go but Mr. Bell said the Capt. engaged the ambulance to go on a social call; I thought that vehicle belonged to your department and is intended for the sick only. So it is, says the Doctor, and I am going to see about it. I said, Doctor, I do not feel well enough to walk three miles and back today. In a few minutes Joe Bell drove up with the ambulance, saying, Ike, get ready, I will drive you to town. So I went before the field Board of Surgeons and Physicians. Dr. Beauchamp had sent in his report of me, and I was pronounced unfit for active duty and discharged from service on account of ill health. This action took me from under the jurisdiction of Capt. Howell, greatly to my relief. I thanked the Board, saying, Gentlemen, I enlisted for the war, and at times I am able to do some duty. There are other duties besides standing guard, camping out and shooting. I am willing to do anything I am able to do. About that time Major Martin came in, undoubtedly sent there by Capt. Howell. After speaking to the Doctors he turned to me, we shook hands and he said, Well Hermann, take good care of yourself, I hope you will recover and get entirely well; you have been badly treated, I am sorry to say. Good bye. We again shook hands, he mounted his horse and departed at a gallop. The Board gave me an order to report to Gen. E. K. Smith, who was then in Atlanta, doing post duty. He asked me how long I had been on the sick list, and I replied about three months. He said, Can you do any office work; I answered I did not know to what kind of work he would assign me to. He said, Can you write? I told him yes; so he put me to copying some documents, which I did to his satisfaction. The desk at which he put me to work was breast high and I had to stand up. The following day I was suffering so I could not do anything, and I had no more medicine. The next day I felt worse. Dr. G.

G. Crawford called in the office; he was in charge of the fair ground hospital. General Smith said, Doctor, what is the matter with this man; since yesterday, he seems to be suffering very much. Dr. Crawford spoke to me and asked what my complaint was. I told him I was suffering in my chest, and I was trying to write at that desk and grew worse. He said, You are a Frenchman? I said Yes. He said he could tell it from my brogue. And he then talked French to me and told me he studied medicine in Paris, and having lived there myself our conversation grew interesting to both of us. So he turned to General Smith and said General, I think I can help him considerably, even if I can't cure him. So General said, "Hermann, you go with Dr. Crawford, he will take charge of you. And we left together for the fair ground hospital, a temporary institution, built of wood, roughly put up, consisting of several wards, whitewashed in and out. I found Dr. Crawford to be a perfect gentleman and very interesting and we got along like brothers; he was very kind to me. Under his treatment I recuperated wonderfully and in a couple of weeks I thought I was entirely cured. I made myself as useful as possible, still continuing my course of medicine. Dr. Crawford appointed me to the same position I held under Dr. Green at the Floyd hospital at Macon, and he was well pleased with my work, as well as the inmates of the hospital.

CHAPTER XX.

General Bragg was removed from the command of the army of Tennessee and Gen. Joseph E. Johnston appointed in his place early in the Spring of 1864. The campaign opened and Gen. J. T. Sherman commanded the Federal forces. His sanguinary and uncivilized warfare on the defenseless is a matter of history. His careless application of the torch, destroying by fire whatsoever he could not carry off, leaving the old and decripid, the women and children to perish in his wake as he marched through Georgia, and reducing to ashes everything within his reach, within a scope of territory fifty miles wide by over three hundred miles long. Johnston's army consisted of only about half the strength of that of his antagonist, consequently he adopted tactics by which he reduced Sherman's army every time that General would make an attack. Joseph E. Johnston acted all along on the defensive, but was ever ready to inflict severe punishment. When General Sherman would force his lines of defense, thus General Johnston generally ceded ground. While his defeats were actual victories, as the cemeteries along the line of his march indicate. The hospitals were filling up with sick and wounded; provisions became scarce, especially as our territory became gradually contracted. So Dr. Crawford came to me one morning, saying, "Hermann, I want to send you out on a foraging expedition. Do you think you can buy up provisions for the hospital? I just drew my allowance of $10,000.00; it wont buy much at present prices." Yes, I can try and make it go as far as possible. What do you say? I remarked, Doctor, I will try and do my best. So he gave me two packages of newly struck Confederate money, all the way from $1,000.00 to $5.00 bills, more money than I had ever had in my possession, and I was actually afraid to carry such sums around with me, although I knew it was not of much value. I also wanted all the linen, lint and bandages that I could get. I came to Washington county where I was known; I put a notice in the weekly paper edited by J. M. G. Medlock, setting forth my mission, and that I would gladly receive any contribution for the sick and wounded at the fair ground hospital in Atlanta, under the charge of Dr. Geo. G. Crawford, of the army of Tennessee, and that I would pay the market price to any who did not feel able to contribute the same free of charge; that I would publish all contributions in the Central Georgian. I wrote to the Central Railroad Company's office at Savannah, asking them to kindly spare me two box cars, one at Bartow and one at Davisboro, on a certain day, when I would load them with provisions for the hospital. The officials kindly offered me the cars free of charge. It was on Thursday I came to Bartow. Mr. Sam Evans, the agent, gave me all his assistance, and provisions commenced to rolling in. Mr. Warren from Louisville, Ga., sent me four horse wagon loads of flour from his mill, free of charge. Mr. Tarver, a large planter, brought me a heavy load of meats, chicken, eggs, butter, etc. Mr. B. G. Smith also brought me a hogshead of hams, shoulders and sides, the meat all nicely smoked, and 100 pounds of leaf lard, chickens, eggs and sweet potatoes, in fact the farmers of that section, all well to do people and slave owners, vied with each other as to who could do the most. I filled up the car that day with the choicest provisions which did not cost me a nickel. Many poor women would bring me the last chicken they had, and when I wanted to pay for the same refused to take the money, and regretted they could not do any more. They unraveled all the old linen table cloth and brought me bags full of lint and bandages. That night I forwarded the car under special instructions by Mr. Evans that it contained perishable goods, labeled for the hospital in Atlanta. The following day I went to Davisboro, Ga. W. C. Riddle, Simon Thomas, Daniel Inman, Ben Jordan, Syl Prince, Daniel Harris and others in that neighborhood proved themselves as generous and patriotic as the people of Bartow and filled my car to overflowing with all kinds of provisions, with the exception of one instance; in regard to his worthy family I will withhold his name. He was a well to do farmer and had a profession. He was a hot secessionist and made speeches to that effect. On the day of receiving he came up in a fine buggy, with a bushel of sweet potatoes. I said to him, What are they worth? He answered, "Four dollars," I think is what they are selling at. I paid the money and he departed, and that was all the money on the debit side of the $10,000.00. The same was published as stated in the Georgian. I returned to Atlanta with the last car of provisions and when I alighted from the car the hospital convalescents actually carried me on their shoulders and would not let me walk. Dr. Crawford looked on me in wonder when I returned my account and gave him back the $10,000.00 minus $4.00, and said, Well that gives me money to fix up my hospital as it should be. He bought sheets and mattresses and had the hospital renovated and made as comfortable as money could make it. Under Dr. Crawford's treatment I again became strong and the paroxisms of pain gradually gave way and became less frequent until I really considered that I was a well man again.

CHAPTER XXI.

My cousin in Macon gave a little social entertainment and sent me an invitation. I showed the same to the Doctor, and he said, Well go, I give you 48 hours. The following morning I hurried to the Quartermaster with my furlough for transportation by placing my permission on his desk. The train just blew the signal for departure; I picked up the transportation and in my hurry left my furlough on the desk. Between Atlanta and Griffin the guards passed through the coaches to inspect all papers of the passengers. When they came to me I found my transportation in my side pocket minus my forty-eight hours leave of absence. I explained how it might have happened, and hoped they would let me continue, but I was requested to get off at Griffin, which I did, and asked the guard to conduct me to the Provost Marshal, so that I might explain, and he could inform himself, never doubting but that he would wire and inform himself of the correctness of my statement and let me proceed. Instead, he told me he had heard such statements before and informed the guard to be especially vigilant in regard to me, so I was conducted to an old livery stable that served as a prison. This was in Dec. 1863. I spoke to my guard if there was not a way by which I could communicate with Dr. Crawford in Atlanta; he said he did not know. I said, Please tell the Provost to write to Dr. Crawford about me. Presently one of the guards brought me a broom, saying, It is a rule when a new comer comes to make him sweep out the calaboose. I said, Well this time you will have to break your rule. Do I understand that you refuse to comply? I certainly do. He went to the Sergt. of the Guard and made his report as to what passed between us. The Sergt. came at once, saying I understand you refuse to sweep out the calaboose. I certainly do; is it for this which I am arrested? He said, Do you know the penalty, sir? No, and I don't care, was my reply. He remarked, You'll be bucked and gagged for two hours. I again said, "You'll have a nice time doing it." He answered. Not so much talk; pull off your overcoat. I said, If I do I'll make you feel sorry for it. All this occurred while I was standing before the fire place, with my hands behind me. In front of me about five feet distance, stood a wooden bench. The Sergeant stood between me and it. Calling for the guard to come up, they asked him if they should bring their guns. He said no, only one bring his gun. They came up. When the Sergeant put his hand on me as if to unbutton my coat. I had moistened the knuckles of my fingers by passing them between my lips, concentrated the muscles' tension and struck the Sergeant over the bridge of his nose, sending him sprawling backward over the bench, his head hitting the pavement, and I had to dodge to avoid his heels hitting me under the chin. The man who had the musket made a lunge at me. Fortunately I had a memorandum book in my side pocket which he hit and dented the leaves of it half way through. I grabbed at the gun and caught it just at the curve of the bayonet, close to the muscle, and jerked it out of his hands. I made moulinets, holding the gun by the barrel and bayonet, and drove the whole guard, consisting of twelve men, before me. One of them stopped at the rack, close to the door, which was open, to reach for a gun, when I hit him with the butt end on the arm, just below the shoulder, and sent him to the ground, falling as he went in the middle of the street. The exit of the men out of the guard house was so hasty it attracted the attention of the populace so that in a very short space of time a crowd had assembled before the door, looking askance as to what had happened, among which was a Lieut. Colonel, judging from the ensign he wore. Advancing to me, who stood quietly at the entrance, at parade rest, he, undoubtedly thinking that I was the sentinel, asked me what was the matter, what are the casualties. I simply remarked, Nobody hurt on my side, Colonel. What is all this assemblage here doing? So I explained to him what had happened and the cause of it. He asked me where were the guards. I pointed out some of them in the crowd; they gradually approached. He asked some of them to lead him to the Provost Marshal, whose name was Capt. Willis, which gentleman (pardon the expression), he berated to the utmost, telling him that he was not fit for a hog herder much less to be in command of human beings, who ever heard of bucking and gagging in the Confederate Army. I am going to report you to the proper authorities, and he ordered him to send me back to Atlanta by the next train, so that I might prove my assertion. The train from Macon to Atlanta was due within half an hour, so I was sent back under guard of a Lieutenant and four men with loaded muskets, with orders to shoot should I make an effort to escape. Luckily in my school days, which were close to an army post, I went twice a week to the armory to take lessons in boxing and sword exercise, and while I do not profess to be an expert in those sciences, they served me tolerably well in the above stated instance, and others through which it has been my misfortune to pass. Arriving in Atlanta, I was conducted to the Provost Marshal. The Lieutenant in command of the guard handed him a letter which the Provost read, after which he looked at me, standing in the middle of the room, and said, Well Lieutenant, I'll take charge of the prisoner; you can go back by the next train. The Lieutenant saluted him and he and his guard departed. It was between four and five o'clock in the afternoon. There were two more men at the office at their desks, and they soon left the room, leaving me and the Provost by ourselves. Turning to me he said, You belong to Walker's Brigade? I said, Yes, Howell's Battery. He said, Well I thought I knew you. He said, Well you got in a h——l of a scrape. I answered that I did not know that a man losing his furlough was so criminal. He looked up at me in surprise, saying, This is not what you are charged with; you are charged with striking a superior officer; do you know the penalty? Yes, shot if found guilty. What did you do it for? About that time I had been eyeing my questioner all along, I thought I knew him but I could not place him. He was Capt. Beebee of a South Carolina Regiment. I answered him thus, "Well, Captain, I fought for the rights of the Confederacy for the last three years and thought five minutes for myself was not too much." I explained to him all of the circumstances leading to my present condition. He exclaimed, "My God, why did you not kill him?" I said I did my best, I only got one lick at him and I give him a good one. He said Go over to the quartermaster's and see if you find your papers; if not I will give you some that will carry you through. I ran across the street, asking the quartermaster if I did not leave my furlough on his desk that morning. He opened a drawer and handed me my paper. I thanked him and reported my find to Capt. Beebee, who said, I know you are alright, you can go. We shook hands and I went my way to the fair ground hospital for the night to make a new start in the morning. Dr. Crawford seeing me said, I thought you had gone to Macon. I answered that I had gone a part of the way and was brought back under guards. How was that? So I recounted to him all the circumstances and illustrated with a musket the picture of the guard getting out of my reach. Dr.

Crawford laughed till he cried. Well you had a time of it said he. I sure did, and half of my permit is out. He said, Well go and stay as long as you like it, but not too long. He wrote me another permit and I again made for the train leading to Macon. This time the guard did not come aboard inspecting papers, but the train on arriving at Griffin was entered by the guards and papers were shown. I was sitting by the window of my coach when I heard some one say "Sergt. there is the fellow, the same fellow," pointing at me. I had not noticed the Sergt. at first as I was looking above and beyond him, and I saw him standing right close beside the train, in front of the window. I put out my head to speak to him; he had a bandage around his forehead and both of his eyes were inflamed and discolored. I said to him, Sergt. are you hurt? He did not reply, so I said, I am sorry for you, the next time you want to have some fun in the bucking, gagging line you try some one else who likes that kind of sport better than I do. The train departed and nobody even looked at my papers that day. I arrived at Macon a day after the feast, but had a pleasant day anyhow.

CHAPTER XXII.

Before the battle of Resaca Dr. Crawford was ordered to move his hospital further into the interior, so he located at Vineville, a suburb of Macon. He pitched his buildings in front of Mr. Burrell Jordan's premises and sent me again on a foraging expedition. I came again home to Washington County, expecting to make headquarters at the home of Mr. Benjamin G. Smith, where I was always welcome. Mr. Smith however, at that time seemed to be very much disturbed and not in his usual pleasant and cheerful mood. I asked him the cause of his troubles; he handed me a slip of paper just received from Lieut. Stone, recruiting agent at Sandersville, to be sure and report without fail at Sandersville on the following Thursday to be mustered into service. Mr. Smith was a widower; his wife had died a couple of years previous, leaving him an only daughter about four years old. Mr. Smith was the owner of about one hunded slaves and a very large plantation. He remarked to me, Hermann, I do not mind going to the front, but what is to become of my dear little Jenny among all those negroes; this is more than I can stand. Mr. Smith was a great benefactor to the indigent widows and orphans, and soldiers families. He contributed unstintedly to the wants of those at home whose male persons were at the front fighting the battles of their country; in fact he run his whole plantation in their interest, making thousands of provisions which he distributed among them as they stood in need and without remuneration. This was the period of the war when everybody able to bear arms was called to the front, and the saying was, "The Government is robbing the cradle and the grave." Sherman was advancing; Johnston was falling back; the people were clamorous for a test fight, General Johnston could not see the advantage of the same and still kept retreating. The battle of Kennesaw mountain was hotly contested, with severe punishment to the enemy but Johnston withdrew and thus fell back to the gates of Atlanta. Referring again to Mr. Smith, I told him I thought I had a solution to his troubles. I said, Carry your little girl to Mrs. Francis, your sister; she will take care of her. This is only Tuesday, we will run up to Macon tonight, and I will plead your cause before Governor Brown, who had established his headquarters there. I think it worth a trial anyway, you can't lose anything by it anyhow. This was about

3 o'clock p. m. He at once gave orders to his cook to boil a ham and make biscuits and that night about midnight we took the train to Macon, Ga. We took breakfast at my cousin's and repaired to the Governor's headquarters. I saw the Governor in front of a table, examining some papers. I said, This is Governor Brown? He said Yes, what will you have? I introduced myself, stating that I was a member of Howell's Battery, and that on account of disabilities was relieved from duty and assigned by Dr. Crawford as foraging agent. I related the condition of Mr. Smith and his surroundings, saying, That man is worth as much at home as a regiment at the front. The Governor at once wrote on a sheet of paper, handing it to Mr. Smith, said, Hand this to the enrolling officer. It was an exemption from military duty. We took our leave, thanking the Governor. Mr. Smith was so overcome with the fact that I had never seen such emotion displayed by a man; tears ran down his cheeks, his thoughts concentrated on his "Sis" as he called his little daughter Jenny.

Mr. Smith lived to a ripe old age. He was of a very benevolent disposition. He was a religious man but not a fanatic, quick answering and very charitable. Many now prosperous and substantial citizens owe their start in life to his munificence. He was as gentle as a woman but as firm as a rock in his convictions. In his death Washington County has sustained an irreparable loss and the State a true and loyal citizen.

CHAPTER XXIII.

General Joseph E. Johnston was removed from command and General John B. Hood was appointed in his stead. Dr. Crawford was ordered to remove to Montgomery, Ala. In reference to the battle of Resaca I omitted to state that I received a letter from my friend B. S. Jordan, whom I had appointed as local agent to forward supplies for the general hospital, that his brother, Jas. P., a Capt. in the 57th Ga. Regt., and a dear friend of mine, was dangerously wounded. I at once set out in quest of him and found him lying on a pallet on the platform of the depot. He was suffering, but when he saw me he brightened up. I said, poor fellow, are you wounded badly? He said, Yes, and indicated the place. Now I have to refer to a little incident that transpired at the time when Capt. Jordan had organized a Company and was about to leave for the front: This was in 1862. When I had already experienced one year's service in the 1st Ga. Regiment. I said, Well, James, don't you let me hear of you being shot in the back. He was indignant. Never, replied he, emphatically. But when he indicated his wound, I remarked at once: Shot in the back, as I expected. Suffering as he was, he laughed heartily and said I want to explain; I said, No explanation is necessary, the evidence is before me. He remarked, Yes, but I want to explain how it was done. I said evidently by a musket ball in the hands of a Yankee, and so I teased him until he nearly forgot all about his wound, which was in the fleshy part of his hip. Captain James P. Jordan was of a noble and chivalrous disposition and his Company had seen much hard service. He explained that they were ordered forward on a double quick to charge the enemy in their immediate front, when owing to some obstructions his Company got out of line, turning towards them to align them a ball had struck him and he was carried to the rear. I carried him to the Vineville hospital. Dr. Crawford extracted the ball, and when his Uncle Burrell heard of his being there he had him removed to his home and well taken care of.

It must be remembered matters were getting very squally; every available man and boy was called to the front. The battle of Atlanta was fought and lost at a great sacrifice to both sides, on July 21st, 1864, Gen. W. H. T. Walker on our side, General McPherson on the Federal side, were both killed. The City was sacked and laid into ruins as a result of the most uncivilized warfare. General Hood changed his tactics, and after the engagement at Jonesboro he swung to Sherman's rear, expecting by that move to cut off Sherman's supplies and reinforcements, and Sherman having now no army in front to oppose him marched through the length of Georgia by rapid strides to the sea, Savannah being his objective point.

CHAPTER XXIV.

The prisoners at Andersonville, amounting to many thousand, owing to their Government refusing to exchange them, preferring to let them die in their congested condition rather than to release those of ours, caused untold hardships on those unfortunate fellows. Their own Government even refused to furnish them with the requisite medical relief and medicine which became unobtainable on account of the close cordon of blockaders guarding our ports of entry. It must be remembered that while we on the Confederate side had only seven hundred thousand available men, in round numbers, in every branch of the service, our adversary had, according to statistics, two million, seven hundred thousand men in the field, and while we had exhausted all our resources they still had the whole world to draw from. Neither were they particular then, as now, as to what kind of emigrants landed in Castle Garden or Ellis Island, but they accepted the scum of the world, paying fifteen hundred dollars bounty as an incentive to enlist in their army. Such were the conditions in the latter part of 1864. General Wheeler's Cavalry was the only force that swung close to Sherman's flanks, thus keeping his columns more compact and preventing them from doing more depredations than they did. Even as it was, they lived on the fat of the land, and as stated, wantonly destroyed what they could not carry along, to the detriment of the defenceless women and children.

Dr. Crawford was ordered to remove his hospital to Montgomery, Alabama. I was out foraging ; I was at Davisboro, Station No. 12, Central R. R. when a train load of the Andersonville prisoners stopped at the station. The train consisted of a long string of box cars. Davisboro was not then the prosperous little city it is now; it consisted of only one dwelling and outhouses usually attached to a prosperous plantation, and a store house; it was owned by Mrs. Hardwick, the great grandmother of our now Congressman, T. W. Hardwick, an elderly widow lady, who for the accommodation of the railroad kept an eating house where the train hands would get their meals as the trains passed on schedule time. Curiosity led me to approach the train, which was heavily guarded by sentinels stationed in the open doors and on top of the cars, with loaded muskets, to prevent escapes, when I heard the grand hailing words of distress from an inmate of the car. Being a Mason, I demanded what was wanted, when some one appealed to me, "For God's sake give me something to eat, I am starving to death; somebody stole my rations and I have not eaten anything for three days." Being meal time I at once run in the dining room of the Hardwick House, picked up a plate with ham and one with biscuits, and ran to the train, called on the man in Masonic terms, and handed him the provisions that I had wrapped up in a home made napkin, bordered with indigo blue. It was seven o'clock p. m. and one could not distinguish the features of an individual; it was a starless, foggy night. After the train left I entered the house and excused myself for the rudeness of taking the provisions as I did. Mrs. Hardwick not having been in the dining room at the time I explained to her that my obligations were such that I had to render assistance to any distressed Brother Mason; he applying to me as such; "I am now ready to pay you for all the damages I did," and this was her reply: "I don't charge you anything honey, I am glad you did it." But not so with her housekeeper, Miss Eliza Jackson, who berated me for everything she could think of, saying, "They had no right to come here and fight us; you are nothing but a

Yankee yourself," etc., etc. Miss Jackson was a long ways beyond her teens, so I said, "Miss Liza, you are mad, because owing to the war your chances for marriage have greatly diminished, especially with the disposition you have." Those present enjoyed her discomfiture.

Usually when troops were about to be ordered in transit, they were issued three days rations, all of which were often walloped out of sight at one square meal on account of its meagerness; undoubtedly that is what happened to my Masonic Brother; he received his rations and someone stole them. I myself often ate at one meal what was intended to last me three days and trusted for the future. I never felt any remorse of conscience to get something to eat, if I could; I felt that the people for whom I devoted my services in those days, owed me a living, and when the authorities failed to supply it, I took it where I could find it.

CHAPTER XXV.

I rejoined Dr. Crawford and he sent me out again. I took the train to Greenville, Alabama, and walked about eight miles to Col. Bowens', who was an uncle of Mrs. John George. Mrs. George was a niece of Mrs. Braswell, where I boarded. She came to spend many days with her Aunt while I was with the family; her home was only about three miles distant. She married Mr. George and moved to Butler County, Alabama. Mr. Bowen, her uncle, furnished me with a horse and I rode out to see them. Butler county is a sort of an out of the way place, and that country had not been overrun with soldiers, and provisions were plentiful. When I hollowed at the gate she recognized me at once and was overjoyed; she took me around the neck and kissed me. George ran out saying, "Mollie! Mollie! What are you doing." She said, "Never mind that is home folks." Poor woman, she was so overcome to see someone from home that she actually cried for joy. They were a happy family. I gave them all the news about their people, as I had just come from there. I stated my business and both of them set in the following day to assist me in my duty. Butler county, where they lived was a very hilly country, but tolerably thickly settled, and provisions came in by the quantities. I, with the assistance of my host and hostess, filled a single box of eggs six by three feet long and three feet high. We stood every one on its end with alternate layers of bran and sawdust and carried them over a very rough road to Greenville, together with a great many chickens and shipped them to the hospital, and we only lost three dozen eggs by breakage. One morning we heard the report that the enemy, in great force, was approaching. People were leaving the city. With the exception of a small garrison there was no defense. Dr. Crawford had to abandon the city, removed all that were in condition to get away, but there were about a half a dozen men who were too sick to be removed. The enemy came into the city soon after we left. Dr. Crawford remarked to me that evening, "Herman, I am going to send you back to take charge of the hospital and those poor fellows that I could not get away." I demurred, saying that I did not care to be taken prisoner. He said, "Listen; In all civilized warfare the medical department is exempt from molestation." I said, "From the way this war is waged it is not altogether civilized, but I am under your orders; I'll do what you want me to do." He said, "I'll take it as a great favor; I can't abandon those poor fellows, some one has to take care of them and administer to their wants." He said he did not know where he would locate but wherever he went I must come back to him. I was then about nine miles from Montgomery. It was late in the evening, and I took it afoot back." When passing through Macon on my way to Montgomery, I passed a night with my cousin, Mrs. Wurzbourg, whose husband was exempt from military duty on account of physical infirmity. My jacket which I wore was threadbare, and even (holy). He presented me with one of his blue flannel sack coats. I had previously been able, through Dr. Crawford, to get enough cloth for a pair of pants and vest. It was blockade goods which the Government had purchased, and it was of a coarse textile, and of a light blue cast, and thus I was fairly decently clothed. In those days the Confederate grey was very much lacking, and men, as well as women, had to wear anything, of any color they could get hold of. So after leaving Dr. Crawford, to return to the hospital at Montgomery, I stopped over at a cottage. The proprietor had a watch repair and jewelry shop in

Montgomery, who owned a small plantation about six miles from the city. He had left the city for lack of business, and now lived at his country home. He was an Englishman, his wife was French. This book being written entirely from memory, after a lapse of about a half a century, I can't remember the names of those people, but they were very kind and hospitable. After supper we repaired to their little parlor. The house was well kept, and proved that the mistress of the same knew how to manage a home and make it comfortable. There was a piano, and I asked the lady, (talking French to her), if she would kindly play a little. So she asked me if I could sing some French songs; I said a few. She at once repaired to the instrument, and asked me what will you have. I of course called for the Marseillaise, which she performed to perfection. So she asked me to sing; I started the melody of

>Adieu Patrie
>France Cherie
>Ou Chaque jour
>Coulait si pure
>Monhelvretie
>Douce et jolie
>Pays d 'Amour
>Ociel d azure
>Adieu, Adieu!

Having finished that stanza I noticed she had quit playing and was crying; so I remarked, "Madam, had I known that my singing would have had such an effect I surely would not have sung." By way of explanation she remarked that her first husband was a composer and that the song I sang was his first effort and he received a prize on it. Oh those were happy days she said! Her husband talked very kindly to her and the general conversation turned on France and of days gone by. She had lived in Paris and knew many business houses that I knew and I passed a most pleasant night. The following morning I sat down to a substantial country breakfast. We had hardly finished when the negro servant ran in, saying, "Master the Yankees are coming. They are here." Looking up the road, sure enough, a few hundred yards beyond where the road turned, they were in view. I at once, on the first impulse, jumped into a closet. Hardly was I in, closing the door, when I thought of this being the first place they would examine. I opened the door, and not knowing where to go I went into the back yard, between the house and the smoke house. Hardly had I done so when a dozen or more Yankees left their column entered the house very boisterously. Being dressed somewhat like they were, in blue, lacking but the brass buttons, I entered the back door, unconcernedly, mixing among them without being detected or noticed. Some of the men had placed their guns in the corner of the room; when of a sudden my hostess run in by the back door, crying, "My God! They are taking all of my meat." I don't know what impelled me but I seized a gun from the corner, ran out of the back door, brought my weapon from a trail to a support, and ordered the two men to throw back the hams each of them had in their grasp, one of which acted at my command, and the other said, What in the h——l you got to do with it. Before I could reply his comrade said to him, "Throw it down, don't you see he is a safe guard;" he threw down the hams. I took the cue from what the Yankee said, although it was the first time I had heard of a safe-guard. The door of the dwelling wide open, those in the house saw me walk the post back and forth, made their exit and left the house, and as long as I was guarding, no more Yankees tarried on the premises; they came, looked about and left the premises as soon as they saw me standing guard, until the whole column had passed. My host came to me saying, Well, they are all gone, thank God, I said no, the rear guard has not passed. The dwelling house was constructed close to the ground, leaving only about a foot space in front while the rear end was about two and a half feet from the ground. I took my gun and crawled under the house. Presently there came what I thought to be about a regiment, and several stragglers. Finally I came from under the house. I gave my hostess the gun I'd taken, telling her, If I do not call for it it shall be yours. My host took my hands, shook them heartily, saying, "You are a hero;" I laughed, saying, Well, I saved your bacon; Good bye; I am much obliged to you for your kind hospitality, and if it had not been for those fellows we would have had a good time. I started on my philanthropic errand, not knowing if I would find the sick men dead or alive. I had gone but a few hundred yards when I met a Federal soldier marching hastily to catch up. He said, Are they far ahead; I said, No, about five hundred yards or a quarter of a mile. You are going the wrong way, said he. I answered, I am not going far, I lost something. Further on I met two more, who like the first, took me for a Federal. One said, Comrade you are going the wrong way. I said, I am not going far. How far behind are we? I said, Not far, a few hundred yards. And so within about one and a half mile I met a dozen stragglers, walking to catch up, all comparatively asking the same questions, and to which I replied alike. When about four hundred yards in front of me, and about alike in the rear of the last straggler I saw four horsemen, riding abreast, holding their carbines by the barrel and resting the butt on their thighs. I recognized them as Confederates. I walked up to them, asking, What troops do you belong to? Harvey's Scouts of Forrests' Cavalry, was their reply. Are there any others behind? Yes. How far? The rear of the enemy's column is about two miles ahead of you, said I, and there are about a dozen stragglers, some with guns, and some have none; they are separated several hundred yards apart, some single and some in pairs; if you spur up you can catch the whole gang; I'll tell those men ahead of me to hurry up. Where is Capt. Harvey? You'll find him in the Exchange Hotel, in town. They at once put spurs to their horses and galloped on, and I followed my course towards the city. I met the reinforcements some little distance ahead of me, and reported what I had seen and told their advance scouts. They all went at full speed, and later, I saw the whole gang of stragglers brought in. I asked Capt. Harvey what had become of the inmates at the hospital. He said he did not know for he had just arrived that morning. I went to the hospital, found things in rather bad shape and the inmates gone. After careful investigation I heard that the Ladies Relief Association had taken care of the sick and that they were well provided for.

CHAPTER XXVI.

Dr. Crawford followed General Hood's army and established headquarters at Corinth, Miss. I followed at once, as soon as I could locate him. I bought what provisions I could along the stations. At Columbus, Miss., some Federals who came there to tear up the track fired in the train as we passed; several of the passengers were wounded but General Forrest appeared at that moment on the scene and routed the enemy, killing and wounding quite a number of them, and thus preventing the wreckage of the railroad track. The car I rode in was riddled with bullets, but I escaped unhurt; several of the passengers had a close call.

While at Corinth I was deputized to carry a message to the front, this side of Franklin, Tennessee. I arrived in time where General Beauford's men had a brush with the enemy. A stray bullet hit me in the thigh, and for a time I thought I was seriously hurt. I was close to a little stream of water. I had my leg tied above the wound with my handkerchief and put it in the running stream. A surgeon came to probe my wound, but trembled like a man having the palsy, and I told him he must not touch me any further; he could hardly put his probe in the hole made by the bullet. After a while I was picked up and sent to the rear where I was cared for by Dr. Crawford, who was very sorry and regretted having sent me. My wound was doing so well and there was no inflammation taking place, and by keeping cold applications on it I was able to be about in less than two weeks. Dr. Crawford said I did the best thing that could be done by keeping inflammation down by putting my leg in the stream. The wound did so well that he would not bother it to extract the ball, and so I still carry it as a memento of the war. While at Corinth the ladies of Washington county sent me a box. The battle of Franklin was fought and a victory dearly bought. Two weeks later the battle of Nashville was fought, and General Hood's magnificent army nearly annihilated. They came through Corinth the worst conditioned men I ever laid my eyes upon. There I met Lieut. John T. Gross of this County and Capt. Joe Polhill of Louisville, Ga., and about twenty of their command. They were hungry and in rags; I said, "Boys, you are in a bad fix." Capt. Polhill said, "Ike, can you tell me where I can get something to eat; I am starved." I said I had just heard that there was a box in the depot for me, let us see what is in it. I took the crowd up to the hospital and all got something to eat. The hospital wagon went to the depot and got the box. It was a large box, and was filled to the top with clothes and eatables. Lieut. Gross, who was barefooted, I supplied with a pair of broken shoes. Many of the provisions were cooked. I took out some checked shirts and knit socks and a pair of pants and jacket and divided the rest among the boys, who were all from Jefferson and Washington counties, and even to this day Capt. Polhill declares I saved his life. He is still one of the Vets. and a useful and honored citizen of Louisville, Ga.

Corinth at that time when I saw it, was only a railroad station with an improvised station house or warehouse. A few chimneys here and there indicated where had previously stood some houses. It is not far from the Tennessee river, about ten miles from Shiloh, where Albert Sidney Johnson, from Texas, was killed and General Beauregard saved the day. During my convalescence I walked over some of the battle ground. Being tired I sat down on a log. There were two logs touching each other lengthways. They had been large trees, about two and a half to three feet in diameter. Playing on the ground with my crutch I unearthed a bullet; presently I scratched up another. I noted that the logs were riddled with bullets. I picked up over one hundred pounds of musket balls in a space not over twenty-five feet square. How any escaped such a shower of lead in such a small place can't be possible. Undoubtedly those logs had served as a protection behind which those brave fellows sent forth in the ranks of their adversaries a similar amount of death dealing missiles.

CHAPTER XXVII.

This brings us towards the last part of December, 1864. When General Hood planned his campaign to the rear of General Sherman, instead of following General Johnston's tactics and thus leaving the balance of the State of Georgia to the tender mercies of our adversaries, who had no mercy or respect for age nor sex, but wantonly destroyed by fire and sword whatever they could lay their hands on, save the booty and relics with which they were loaded. Howell's battery, on account of their horses being exhausted, could not follow General Hood's army into Tennessee, and were ordered to Macon to recruit. This Company had seen arduous service from Chickamauga to Atlanta, including Jonesboro. After the battle of Chickamauga, one of the hardest contests of the war, in which the confederate forces were successful, Howell's battery had the honor to open the battle from the extreme right, on the 18th day of September, 1863. On the 19th, which was on Saturday, the fight was progressing furiously, with no results, both armies holding their own, but on Sunday morning our forces centered their attack on the enemy's center, charged through their lines and rolled them back in complete disorder, and the victory was ours. General Bragg rested his forces for a few days and renewed the fight around Chattanooga, Lookout Mountain and Missionary Ridge. He found the enemy well fortified and ready. The battle was a sanguinary one; Howell's battery besides losing two pieces of artillery, which were recovered in the evening and returned to us, lost in wounded, Leonidas Hines, Frank Bailey and Corporal Braswell, and captured James Mullen, John S. Kelley, John Tompkins and John Braswell. That night General Bragg withdrew as quietly as possible and went into camp at Dalton, where we spent in winter quarters. At Macon they did provost duty under direction of General Howell Cobb. The writer drifted back through Alabama expecting to rejoin Dr. Crawford as soon as he would locate, and being intercepted by Federal troops I reported to the nearest Confederate post, which proved to be General Beaufort from Kentucky, a cavalry officer at Union Springs, Alabama. General Abe Beaufort was of colossal stature and an able officer, so I reported to him for duty until I could join my proper command. He said, Have you a horse? We are cavalry. I said, No, but I expect to get one the first fight we get into. He laughed and

said, Well, you can hang around here. I stayed
at his quarters several days. One day he seemed
to be worried more than usual; I ventured to
say, "General, You seem to be worried over
something." He said, "I have enough to worry
about; there is General Forrest at Selma; I have
sent him two couriers and neither of them have
reported; I don't know what became of them,
whether they have been captured, killed or run
away. I want to hear from General Forrest so
that we can act in concert of action." The Federals who held possession of Montgomery under
General Wilson's corps d'army, who later captured President Jefferson Davis in Irwin County, Ga., during the several days of my hanging
around at General Beaufort's Headquarters, he
asked me how long I had been in the service. I
said, "I joined the first Company that left my
county and the first regiment that left my
State." How long had you been in this country before the war broke out? I answered that I
came to Georgia direct from France in the Fall
of 1859, about sixteen months before I enlisted.
I found in this country an ideal and harmonious
people; they treated me as one of their own; in
fact for me, it was the land of Canaan where
milk and honey flowed. In the discussion of the
political issues I felt, with those that I was in

contact with, that they were grossly imposed upon by their Northern brethren and joined my friends in their defence, and so here I am, somewhat worsted, but still in the ring. I said, General I have an idea; I think I can carry a dispatch that will land. I have in my possession at home my French passport. I can write for it and use it by going squarely through their lines, as being an alien. I can change my clothes for some citizens clothes. After a little reflection General Beaufort said, "Hermann, you are an angel; it's the very idea." So we arranged to write at once for my pass. It came in due time. The lady of the house where the General kept his quarters furnished me with a suit of jeans cloth, but begged the General not to send me for fear I might meet with reverses. But the General said, He is all right, he can work the scheme. That night I started about ten o'clock, on horseback, with two escorts. It was a starlight night. We passed for some distance through a dense swamp. The General cautioned me to be careful and on the lookout, an admonition I thought entirely unnecessary. He said the enemy's camp was about twelve miles distant, and that they had a company of scouts out that night, and so had we, but as we journeyed along at a walk the lightning bugs were so thick as to blind a fellow and the swamp so dark that we could only designate the road by the distance and open space of the tree tops and the stars. We did not however, meet any of the scouts. On emerging from the swamp I noticed on my right a small farm cottage and a dim light through the cracks of the door, I dismounted, knocked at the door. At first no one answered. I knocked again when a lady's feeble voice answered, Who is there? A friend, was the reply. Open the door please. The door opened and there stood in front of me an old lady of about seventy, I judged, nearly scared to death, trembling from head to foot. To re-assure her I said, Madam, we are Southerners don't be frightened, we won't do you any harm. Can you tell me how far it is from here to the enemy's camp? She answered very excitedly that she had nothing to do with the war, she is only a lone woman and we can't cheat her out of many years. You all have stolen all my meat and did not leave me a mouthful of corn or meat, and I am left here to starve to death. I said, But we are Confederates; but I noticed the woman did not believe me, undoubtedly owing to my brogue, as there were thousands of foreigners in the federal army. I lit a match and scrutinized the ground and noted the doors of the outhouse wide open, houses empty and the

The Capture of the Federal Cavalrymen.

ground churned into dust by the horses hoofs. Undoubtedly we were not far from the enemy, as they were there that day and looted the premises. I bid the lady good night and joined my escort who waited for me in the road. As I was about to mount my horse I perceived ahead of me through the limbs of the trees, a bright light. The lady was still standing in the door, and I asked her what that light was we saw ahead of us. She said they were the negro quarters about a quarter of a mile ahead, and I thanked her and we moved a little forward and held consultation as to what was best to do, whether they should return to camp leading my horse back and I to take it afoot or whether we had better go together to the quarters, probably they might get a few potatoes and some buttermilk, for be it understood that we belonged to the hungry army where rations became very scarce, for as a rule the Confederate soldier respected private property and often suffered hunger rather than appropriate property belonging to others. They concluded they might buy something to eat from the darkies. The negroes in those days, as before the war, always had a surplus of provisions. They were well fed, in fact most of them made their own provisions with the exception of meat, their owner allowing them patches and giving them time to cultivate the same for their own use or to sell with their master's permission, which was generally only a matter of form or respect.

CHAPTER XXVIII.

In keeping my eyes to the front watching the light, we came to an open field on the right. On the left of the road was a dense forest. I noted some one crossing the light and heard some one screaming and hollering like negroes carousing. Presently the same person recrossed and I thought there must be some Federals about there and we stopped to consult. I conclude that I would take it afoot and reconnoiter while my escort would enter the woods where we stood and wait for me until I returned. I took the darker side of the road along the woods until I arrived close to the premises, and I circumvented the place. I noted a double pen log house with a large chimney at one end and a rousing lightwood fire in it. A step over fence about five rails high surrounded the yard in which stood a very large oak tree, the limbs of which hung low, a little above a man's head. To those limbs were hitched three splendid horses. In the house were three Federals, enjoying their surroundings. The house had a front and back entrance and the fire in the chimney cast its light some distance, front and rear, around the premises. I hurried back to my comrades and made my report as above, and I suggested a line of action as follows: We will leave our horses on the road side, about two hundred yards this side the house. One of us will enter the back side as I enter the front, and one of you follow me; Are you willing. If you do as I say we will capture those fellows without firing a shot. The youngest of the escort was a young man of about 19 years; the other was 21 years old. The younger said, General Beauford told us to obey your orders, and I am ready to do what you tell me to do. I said, Bravo, my boy. The other one was silent, I remarked, what do you say? He tried to answer but his teeth chattered and he was trembling so he could hardly speak. I said, What is the matter with you, are you scared? He said, No, I am excited. You must compose yourself if you follow my advice and do exactly what I say and we will capture those fellows without firing a gun, but there must be no wobble, or they may turn the joke on us. I told the youngest to hold his gun ready for use and to make a detour around the house and face the back entrance, and I would give him time to get in position, and as I enter the front door he must enter the back door, and we must get the drop on them, otherwise they might get it on us. I told the other fellow to follow me and do as I do and not to fire unless I do. I carried a couple of colts pistols. As we entered the negro women and the men were sitting on benches before the fire, when I exclaimed, surrender! in the meantime covering them with my pistols and the guns of my comrades. They jumped as if lightning has struck them. "Unbuckle your weapons or you are dead men; be quick about it." My orders were executed with alacrity and we marched them out of the house. In the far end of the house I spied a plow line hanging from a nail in the wall. I appropriated the same and we unhitched the horses and walked to where ours were. Not a word was spoken by either of us. The horses were brought forward and the prisoners mounted. The plow line served to pinion their legs under the animals below. All this was done as quickly as possible. When the prisoners realized that we were but three, one of them commenced being obtrusive and talking loud and abusive. I cautioned him and his comrades that unless they moved along quietly and not talk above a whisper we would be compelled to leave them by the roadside, for some one, unknown to us, to bury them. My admonition had a good effect, and our cavalcade advanced in a lope, one leading the horses, the prisoners were riding by the bridle reins, and

I and the other man closing up the rear. I was fearful of meeting some of their scouting parties, of which General Beaufort advised me of on our departure, but it seemed that they were in some other direction from us, for we noted the firmament in every direction lit up by an aurora borealis from the burning houses those miscreants set afire. When arriving close to our pickets we halted. I sent one of my escort in advance to announce our arrival so as not to be fired into, as it was only day break and still too dark to be recognized. I rode at once to General Beaufort's headquarters to report. He was still in bed; the guard admitted me. He said, I thought you were on your way to Selma. I said, General, I met with an accident and came back. An accident said he! So I stated that accidentally I captured three Federals and got me a horse at my first opportunity. He got up and dressed, had the prisoners brought before him and commenced questioning them but they were very reticent and evaded many of his questions. General Beaufort was very anxious to find out the strength of his adversary in his immediate front and their destination. I suggested that I change my clothing for the uniform of one of the prisoners who was my size, and ride in their line. He said, That is a very dangerous business; if you are trapped they will hang you. I said, I am in for the war; life as it is is not worth much, I'll take the chances. So that night after midnight I passed again our videttes, in company with two escorts who accompanied me for company sake for a few miles, when they returned to camp and I went it alone. After passing the cottage of the old lady where we sought information, the previous night, I put my horse at full speed and passed the negro quarters. No one was astir and I continued my course for about three miles when I saw some obstruction in the road on the brow of the hill. Halt, was the command. I halted, at within about seventy-five yards. Who comes. A friend. Seeing that I was alone I was asked to advance. As I approached I noted that there was a rail fence across the road, behind which were two sentinels, their muskets pointing at me. I remarked as I crossed the fence, Didn't I have a race; those four rebels run me clean to nearly where I am. My horse was steaming wet. I said, You see that fire yonder; we set the gin house afire when the rebels came up and gave me a hot chase. The sentinels were all excitement and kept their eyes to the front. I had dismounted and placed myself in line with them. I could have killed them both but that was not my object. Finally, seeing no one coming, I said they must have gone back. I mounted my steed and slowly rode up, in a walk, where I saw what I thought was the main camp, but it was only what was known as the grand guard of about a half a regiment of cavalry. Taking in the surroundings at a glance I noted the horses hitched in the corners of the fence along the road and the men some lying, some sitting on improvised seats around their camp fire. I at once rode to an empty corner in the fence and hitched my horse and walked to a fire where most of the men were lying down, seemingly sleeping. There lay one empty blanket on the ground and I laid myself down on it, facing the fire, which felt pretty good, for I was chilled, the night being cold. As I pretended to take a nap some fellow gave me a hunch with his foot, saying, Hello comrade, you are lying on my blanket. I grunted a little and turned some further when he pulled the blanket from under me. This seemingly roused me, and I was wide awake. I stretched out my arms as if I were yawning, addressing myself to the men next to me, "This is a terrible life to lead. Where are we going? To Savannah. I heard some say Savannah. That is in Georgia, a long ways from here; I am afraid some of us will never get there; I heard that there is an army of fifteen thousand rebels ahead of us within fifteen miles of here." He answered, That would not amount to much with what we have. I thought I would stretch as far as I could reasonably do so, for General Beauford's force was only 1,500 strong. You say that would not amount to much with what we have to oppose them? He said Wilson's Corps amounts to nearly 25,000. O, not that much. He commenced to enumerate different regiments, the number of cannon, etc., etc. All at once I heard the bugle blast "Call to Horse," and everything was active. What's the matter I said, seeing everybody catching their horses? He answered, Did you not get three days rations? I said, Yes. Well we are going to advance. I run to my horse and mounted. I felt that I had to advise General Beauford of this move, and not to pass the picket post that I did coming in I took down the railroad track which run parallel the wagon road some distance, but to my surprise there was a vidette post there of two sentinels. They halted me, saying, You can't pass. I remarked that they will be relieved in a few minutes, that our forces are advancing. There being a nice spring of water in sight, just to the left of the road I wanted to fill my canteen full of water. The road being very dusty I suggested that I would fill theirs if they wished me to in the meantime. I'll be back in a few seconds. So they handed me their canteens and I put the spurs to my horse. Further on I turned to the left into the wagon road and post haste and at full gallop rode into our camp, which was twelve miles ahead of me. The cap which I had borrowed from one of our prisoners was a little too big for my head and in my haste to reach camp blew off. I did not stop to pick it up, but reached camp in about three quarters of an hour. It still being a little before day a bullet passed me in close proximity and I knew that I was close to our lines. I stopped and held up both hands. The bad marksmanship of the sentinel saved me from being shot. I at once rode up to the General's quarters, was admitted by the sentinel and made my report. He was still in bed, but he got up and ordered two companies of Col. Armistead's Regiment to the front and deployed into a skirmish line. In less than an hour we heard the firing. All the forces were astir, and we withdrew towards West Point, Georgia, thus giving the enemy the right of way. The General asked me if I held any commission. I said, Yes, high private in the rear ranks.

Well, I'll see that you will be promoted when I make my report to the war department. I need a hundred men just like you.

CHAPTER XXIX.

That evening I donned my disguise as a citizen, and advanced, as before, to go through their lines as an alien. I rode as before as far as my judgment would permit to prevent the capture of my escort, when I took it afoot to carry out the program first suggested. I walked about four miles and day was breaking. As two nights previous, the country indicated depredations by fires. When I again, as the night before, saw obstructions in front of me, I walked within twenty-five or thirty paces up to it when I was commanded to halt and challenged as to who comes there, their muskets pointing at me. I said, "Me no speaky English, je parle Francais." Where are you going? Me no stand English. They made me a sign to sit down by the side of the obstructive fence, after having let me cross their barricade. About fifteen minutes later an officer with the relief guard came up. Who's that you got there? How did he get here? They answered I walked up. He is a foreigner and can't speak our language. Turning to me he said, where are you going? "Je ne comprenspas, je parle francais." So he made me signs to follow him, which I did. He conducted me to a large camp fire where I saw several men guarding others and recognized them to be Confederates. This was the first time I felt my danger; I was afraid that there might be some among the prisoners that might have seen me before and might recognize me. However my fears were without cause as I did not know any of them. About eight o'clock a. m., the Provost Marshall General came around and addressed himself to me. Who are you, said he. As before, I said je parle francais. Oh, you are a Frenchman. Well, I will get some one that can speak to you. He ordered one of the guards to go to a Canadian Company and ask the Captain to send him a man that could speak French and English. Presently a young soldier presented himself. The Provost took him aside and I pretended not to notice them. They stepped to within a few paces of me; when I heard the Provost say to him, Pump him. I thought, He will be welcome to all he will get out of me. He stepped up to me and talked to me in French. I appeared to be so glad to meet one I could talk to, that I did not give him an opportunity to ask me a single question. I told him how I came here in the fall of 1859, pulling out my passport which he scrutinized and handed over to the

Provost, who in turn looked at the same. I told him that I made a mistake coming here, that the people made it very unpleasant to me because I would not enlist; that I had to leave Georgia, and I am now on my way to New Orleans, which I heard the port was open so as to see the French consul to assist me back to France; that I am tired of this land where people murder each other. During all of our conversation the Provost said, What does he say. My interlocutor explained and then they all would laugh. Finally I said that I was hungry, that I had had nothing to eat in 24 hours. So the Provost said, Boys, can you fix up something for him among you, and they all contributed some from their rations and filled my haversack full of substantial food, and besides contributed $10.00 in money. I thanked them and started off, after being told that I could go, but as I was apparently green I asked my questioner how far I was from New Orleans and if there were any more places where I might be delayed, when the Provost intervened with his, What did he say? Which after being explained to him, he said, I had better give him a pass, they might take him up on the other end of the line, and so he wrote on a slip of paper, "Pass the bearer through the line," and signed his name in such chirography that I could not read it. I arrived into Montgomery late that afternoon, and reported, as per previous arrangement with Col. Paul to Judge Pollard, whose daughter he married, and told that family how the boys were getting along. Judge Pollard was a stately old gentleman of great prominence in that section of the country. He received me in his large library and we had quite a long conversation over the situation. I told him that I was directed to him with the understanding that he would provide me with a horse so that I might continue my journey to Selma. He shook his head and said I'll see what can be done, but I don't believe there is a horse to be got within ten miles of here; the Yankees stole every horse and mule they could lay their hands on, and sure enough he was unable to furnish me with an animal, but thought I might, by making a long detour beyond the flanks of the enemy's columns, be able to proceed. That morning one of the ladies presented me with a tobacco bag, made out of a piece of pink merino, and the initials of my name embroidered on it with yellow silk and filled with smoking tobacco, and a shaker pipe stuck in it. It was quite a novelty and was highly appreciated. After having partaken of a substantial breakfast I bid my host and his family good bye, visited my friends Faber, Lewellen, Coleman and other acquaintances of the city, all of which had their tales of woe and sufferings to account at the hands of the enemy. I departed for Selma on foot. I was weary and depressed. I heard that I was again in close proximity to the enemy who routed Forrest from that city and came within a fraction of either killing or capturing him. He was surrounded by four troopers who demanded his surrender, when he threw his saber, spurred his horse and run the gauntlet among a shower of bullets. I heard that in the melee he received a saber cut in the face. I felt sick at heart and physically worn out and took a rest and wended my way to Col. Bowen,, who was glad to see me and offered me all the comforts to recruit my strength. I remained there nearly a week. I really did not know where to report to, General Beauford being on the retreat before Wilson's corps who came from via Pensacola, Florida. I was surrounded on every side, so I concluded to retrace my way back to Montgomery but when a few miles from Greenville as I emerged from a long lane at the end of which the road turned into a forest I noted some Federal soldiers. I came within a very short distance of them before seeing them; my first impulse was to run back, but I was tired, it being a warm day and nothing to protect me from the bullets, having an open lane where they might play at my fleeing figure. I concluded to give up on demand, but on close approach, seeing that they were negro troops I regretted not having taken chances, however great, of escape, especially when I was asked to surrender my arms, which consisted of a couple of colts 6 inch pistols, one of which I carried in a scabbard buckled around me and the other in the belt of my pants, which were tucked in my boot legs. In unbuckling my belt I contracted my body allowing the one in my pants to slide down my leg into my boot and thus only surrendered one of them. The other I carried on as I marched. The friction of the barrel on the ankle of my foot gave me excruciating pains but I continued on until I could feel the blood on the inside of my boot. There were other prisoners, among them General Pillow and his son, George. Arriving in Montgomery we were locked up in the Lehman Brothers building which had served as a shoe factory for the Confederate Government. I intended to use my weapon at the first opportunity I saw to gain my liberty. That night I asked for a doctor to dress my wounded foot. He came and asked me how that happened. My socks adhered to the wounds and the pains it gave me were unbearable. I told him I had snagged myself. He dressed my wound and I felt relieved to a great extent. The next morning I sent word to my friend Faber to come to see me and he did so. I said to him to see if he could not get me a parole, after he had told me that he had had some Yankee officers quartered at his house, saying that they were all Western men and seemed to be clever fellows. He promised to use his influence. Presently he returned with an officer and I was turned out on parole, but to report every morning at nine o'clock. The following morning I reported, when the officer commanded one of the men to take charge of me and lock me up. I thought the jig was up, that probably I had been reported by some one and that I might fare the worst for it. There were fifty prisoners; we were all called out to form into line and from that into column, and marched up the hill to the capitol, where we received some salt pork and hard tack to last us three days. We were informed that we would be sent to Ship Island, a country of yellow fever, close to New Orleans in retaliation of Andersonville, there to take the chances to live or die; undoubtedly they would have preferred the latter. About one o'clock p. m. a courier rode up to the capitol, followed by another. Presently we were informed that the war was over, that General Lee had surrendered and that Lincoln was assassinated and instead of being sent to Ship Island we were to be paroled under promise not to take up arms again against the United States, until properly exchanged. This brings us up to the early part of June 1865, or latter part of May.

CHAPTER XXX.

Thus it will be noted that while the war was over in the East, we of the Western army didn't know it and were still fighting, all communication between the two armies being cut off. My friend Faber, who was one of the most popular citizens of Montgomery was afterwards elected Mayor of the City. The following morning I prepared to wend my way back to Georgia. My foot was inflamed and gave me pain, so I said to a Yankee Sergeant who was in waiting on some of the officers there if he could not manage to get me some piece of a horse to ride as I was a long ways from home and in a crippled condition. He said, Yes, if I would give him my watch, which was an open faced, old fashioned English lever, generally called bulls-eye. I acquiesced. We marched down one of the main thoroughfares. We halted before an establishment which was used as a guard house and previously had served as a store. In its front on the sidewalk was a cellar. The Sergeant asked them to bring out that horse, and in the meantime asked me for the watch. Thinking of him as a clever, sympathetic soul, owing to his prompt offer of assistance, I unhesitatingly handed him my watch. They having entered the cellar, they lifted out of its confines a frame of horse so poor that six men took him bodily and placed him on the sidewalk. He was actually nothing but skin and bones; I was astonished that life could have existed in such a frame. I said, Is this the best you can do for me? He said, I promised you a horse for your watch and here he is, and he left me. The men were amused at my discomfiture. I finally concluded that a bad ride is better than a good walk and I made the best of a bad bargain. I asked the men if they could get me a bridle and saddle. They answered that they had none, so I made me a halter out of the rope around his neck, pulled off my coat as padding on either side of his sharp backbone so as to serve me as a saddle and asked the man next to me to give me a lift, and there I was, mounted, representing the picture of Don Quixote to perfection. I urged the horse forward and the men hollered Whoa! which command he was only too eager to obey, I eventually got away from that place and took the Eufaula route homeward. It was four o'clock in the afternoon and I was only four miles from my starting point. The animal had neither eat nor drunk anything while in my possession and from his looks probably not in several days previous.

I saw as I passed along at a snail gait, a corral by the side of the road, with all kinds of contraband. There were negroes, women and children, cattle of all description and a quantity of mules and horses, all encircled by a large rope and guarded by sentinels. I passed a soldier about a half mile from this place. I said to him, What troops are those on the right hand side up the hill? He said they were cavalry. I concluded to ride up, that probably I might induce the officer to exchange animals with me so as to enable me to get along, for I came to the conclusion to abandon my steed and take a bad walk in preference to a bad ride. As I approached the camp I noticed a man sitting on a camp stool, his back towards me, his feet propped up against a large tree, reading a newspaper and seemingly greatly preoccupied as he did not hear my approach. He was in negligee, it being a very warm day; he wore nothing but his pants and a spotted white blouse shirt and was bareheaded. I left my horse by the side of a stump and slid off, approaching within a respectful distance in his rear, I said, Good evening. He jumped like he had been shot. I said excuse me sir, I did not mean to scare you. So he peremptorily said, What will you have? I answered, **Are you the commander of these troops?** He said, Yes; what will you have? I answered that I was a paroled prisoner on my way home; that I was crippled and had a long ways to go. The horse I got I bought from one of the Federals for a silver watch. It took me a whole day to get from the City to where I am; that I had noted, coming along, a corral with many loose horses and mules and I ventured to see if he would not be kind enough to furnish me with a better mount than the one I possessed. He replied, What country are you from? I am from France. How long have you been in the army? Ever since the war started. Were you forced into the army or did you volunteer? I volunteered sir. And you have been fighting us for over four years and now come and ask me for a favor? You need not grant it; good bye. And off I hobbled to where I left my horse taking him by the mane I led him up to the stump and was about to mount when the officer commanded me, Come back here, said he, I like your style. You are the first one I've met but what was forced into the army. Tell the officer in charge of the corral to exchange animals with you. I remarked, Colonel, a written order from you might have a better effect. He laughed, got up and walked into his tent and when he returned he handed me a slip of paper addressed to Capt.

Ledger, and read as follows: Exchange animals with the bearer; Col. York, Com'd'g 7, Indiana Cavalry. I thanked him, gave the military salute and retraced my steps towards the corral. I presented my note to the Capt. in charge; he said, Pick out the one you want. There were some excellent animals but many were galled and not serviceable for any immediate use. I spied a medium sized, plump mule. She was in excellent order, and as I was short in funds I thought I could tether her out to eat grass and thus progress without having to buy food. So I took the mule. I asked him if he would furnish me with a saddle and bridle, and he let me have nearly a new Mexican saddle and bridle and I was once more in good shape. Capt. Ledger asked me where I was going. I said, Home, in Georgia. Which way? I am on my way to Eufaula. So he said, I believe I'll ride a piece of the way with you. He had his horse caught, which was a magnificent animal. Riding along side by side I remarked, Captain that is a splendid horse you are on. He said, Yes, I have a pair, you could not tell one from the other; they are spirited animals but perfectly gentle. Their owner must have prized them highly; some of the men picked them up. That's a new name for stealing, said I. He remarked,

I suppose so, but if I could find out their owner I am going to return them to him; I am making some effort towards it. I said, Well sir, it does me good to hear you say so, and to know that there are some men of feeling, and gentlemen among your army. He said, Well, war is war. It is true that many acts were committed unnecessarily harsh, but I am glad it is over and I hope we will all be friends again. He stopped, saying, Well, I have ridden far enough, and I am going back. We shook hands, he wished me a safe journey and cantered back to his camp. It was already late and I proceeded as far as Fort Browder and stopped over night with Mr. Tom Wells. His wife was also a Georgian and a kinswoman of the Braswell family.

CHAPTER XXXI.

The following morning after bidding my host good bye I took the road to Union Springs. On my way I caught up with General Pillow, who was riding in a carriage drawn by two fine mules, and his son George, who was riding horseback. I said, Hello! On your way home? He answered, Yes. What route are you going? We are trying to make Union Springs for tonight; father is not very well and we are making short stations. I remarked, I am surprised they left you your horse. He said, They left us our side arms and let father have his carriage and mules and me my horse. I rode up to the carriage, shook hands with the old General, whose head was as white as snow, congratulated him on his good luck of being able to keep his outfit. He said, Yes, it was more than I expected. We traveled together for several miles when we were met by five men, one of which, a rather portly fellow, remarked, Boys, if this is not Sal, I'll be hanged. And he advanced and took my mule by the bridle, saying, This mule belongs to me, you will have to get off. I said, I reckon not, drawing my pistol. He said, The Yankees stole that mule from me. I said, Well,

I got her from the Yankees, but she cost me a watch worth about thirty dollars. I stated facts as they were, saying, I am on my way to Eufaula and I am crippled and can't walk, and I shall ride there if it costs me my life. So General Pillow interfered, saying, Gentlemen, this is a Confederate soldier on his way home; he is crippled and can't walk. I will pay you for the mule to end the matter. What kind of money? Confederate, of course, I have no other. Well, that is not worth a curse. That is all I've got. The men were still standing in front of me and occasionally touched the reins, when I cocked my pistol, saying, Turn that bridle loose, I am going to Eufaula on this mule. After that I do not care what becomes of it; I expect to take the boat there for Columbus. He answered, I tell you what I'll do; here is a gold chain; I suppose it is worth as much as your watch. I will give you that chain and you'll leave the mule with the hotel man and I'll get her there. So I said all right, when General Pillow remarked, Gentlemen, undoubtedly you are in search of stock; suppose you were to find any that belongs to somebody else, which it would be pretty apt to be, and the owner would come and claim it; would you turn it over to him? The spokesman hesitated, then said, I don't know if I would or not. I said, well, our arrangement suits me; what is the hotel keeper's name? He told me but I have forgotten it. So we arrived at our destination about one hour by sun and stopped all night at the house of Major Pemperton, a friend of General Pillow's. George and I occupied the same bed. He proved to be an excellent companion and we recounted many incidents to one another. After breakfast we parted company. I took the route to Eufaula, Ala., by myself, leaving General Pillow and his son with our host, with whom they proposed to stay for a few days, before continuing their homeward journey, which was near Franklin, Tenn. I arrived at Eufaula at about three o'clock p. m. and inquired for the hotel, whose proprietor I found sitting in a chair in front. Is this the hotel? Yes sir. A soldier on his way home? Yes sir. This is a good mule you have got; will you sell her? I said, How much will you give me for it? He remarked, I have only Thirty-Five Dollars, in Mexican silver and some Confederate money that nobody takes about here. I'll give you the Mexican dollars for the outfit. You will also give me my dinner and fill my haversack with provisions to last me home? Yes, I'll do that too. What time will the boat leave for Columbus? At four o'clock. Well, I have time to take dinner. I turned the mule over to him, he had me served something to eat and paid me thirty-five Mexican silver dollars. I took the chain, which was not gold but galvanized brass, and said, I am glad I have made connection with the boat, I will get home sooner. Handing the proprietor the chain, I said, There is a gentleman who may call for me; you tell him I made connection and went on. This chain belongs to him and I want him to have it. All right, said he. The boat, according to schedule, left for Columbus with me aboard. In Columbus I met Dr. Mullin, a friend of Dr. Crawford's, but could get no information as to his whereabouts. From Columbus I traveled to Atlanta. The sight that met my view was sickening. Instead of a nice little city, for it must be remembered that Atlanta at that time was not the cosmopolitan of this day, it could not have had over seven or eight thousand inhabitants; there it lay in ashes, the work of vandalism. The brick chimneys marked the places where comfortable shelters used to stand. Its inhabitants fled from the approaching foe, fearing even a worse fate at the hands of such unscrupulous barbarians. From Atlanta I followed in the wake of Sherman's army towards Macon, and had it not been for my trade with the hotel keeper of Eufaula to have my haversack filled, I could not have existed to the end of my journey. As already stated, the Country for miles in every direction was sacked and burned. I say this much for the New England civilization, of these days, that in no country, civilized or uncivilized, could such barbarism have excelled such diabolical manifestation. I arrived in Macon at dusk, intending to pass the night at my cousin's. In front of the Brown House came an ambulance, said to contain President Jefferson Davis. They traveled at a good trot, surrounded by a body of cavalry which I was informed were Wilson's men, Macon being in the hands of that General to whom General Howell Cobb surrendered that city. I was sick at heart at our entire helplessness and complete prostration. I called on my relatives who were glad to see me again among the living. They were much depressed at the condition of things, hoping for the best, but expecting the worst. I met Mr. Kaufman, General Cobb's orderly, as I was about to leave for what I called home. I stated that if there was a chance for me to get something to ride it would greatly facilitate my locomotion. My ankle, although still sore was healing nicely. Mr. Kaufman said, I will sell you my horse, I have got nothing to feed him on. I said, I will give you all the money I got for the mule, having given them already the history of my itinerary from Montgomery to Macon. He accepted my offer and I was again in a traveling condition. All along my route devastation met my view. I could not find sufficient corn to give my horse a square meal. Wherever I found a green spot I dismounted to let my horse eat grass. I traveled at night as well as in the day time and arrived at my destination about 10 o'clock a. m. the next day.

CHAPTER XXXII.

Conditions there were not as bad as I had seen along the line of march, although they were bad enough. Mr. and Mrs. Braswell received me as if I had been one of their own family. I found the premises badly dilapidated, fences down everywhere and everything in disorder, the negro men gone, following the yankee army, the negro women and children were still left to be taken care of by their Master and Mistress. Before leaving the Yankees started to set the premises on fire but the servant intervened and begged for their good master and mistress and they desisted in their intentions. I asked if old Sallie could wash my clothes I had on, and if I could borrow something to put on while mine was in process of cleaning, for the enemy had stolen my trunk and its contents and I had no change of garments. Mr. Braswell was of very corpulent stature. fully six feet high, weighing about 250 pounds, while I, in my emaciated condition only weighed 135. One of his garments would have wrapped twice around me. At 12 o'clock dinner was announced, and I was surprised at the good and substantial meal that was served. The menu consisted of fried ham and eggs, corn bread, biscuits, butter and honey. I said, "folks, you ought not to complain; if you had gone through where I have and seen what I have seen you would feel like you live like royalty, for I have seen women and children scratch in the ground for a few grains of corn for sustenance where the enemy's horses were camped and fed." Mr. Braswell then explained how he managed when he heard of the enemy's approach. He took his cattle, horses and mules and everything he could move, deep in the Ogeechee swamp, leaving only a few broke down around his premises which the enemy, General Kilpatricks cavalry, shot down and left for the buzzards. Mrs. Braswell asked me what I was going to do. I said I did not know; I was in hope to meet Cousin Abe Hermann, but you say he was taken prisoner. Do you know where they carried him to? They answered, No, that Cousin Abe was drafted and went as a sutler in General Rube Carswell's regiment and was captured by the enemy and that they had heard nothing from him, direct. Then Mr. Braswell said, As long as I've got a mouthful I will divide with you. We are poor and I don't know how to begin with the new order of things, all the hands having left me. After telling Mrs. Braswell about her kindred in Alabama and of my ups and downs during that afternoon, I spent a sleepless night, ruminating in my mind as to what to do. The future looked dark, the country was ruined. Wherever I cast my eyes, conditions looked the same. The following morning after breakfast I approached Mr. Braswell, saying, My friend, I can't accept your proposition to be an extra burden to you in your already impoverished condition. He said, What are you going to do? I said, The next time you hear from me I will be in a position to make a support, or I will be a dead cock in the pit. I am going to leave this morning. I left for Sandersville, where I met many friends. While there I heard of some of the boys having picked up an abandoned Confederate wagon. There were about fifteen that claimed a share in it. The next day I went to Milledgeville and stopped this side at Mr. Stroters, who had run a distillery during the war. I said, Mr. Stroter have you any whiskey on hand? He said, Yes, one barrel, I had it buried. Can I get about five gallons? He said, Yes. What will you take for it? Five dollars a gallon, in Yankee money, the Confederate money is no good now. I said, I'll take five gallons if you have a keg to put it in. I have no money of the description you want, but I will leave you my horse in bond.

Early in the morning I proceeded on my way to Macon, carrying the five gallon keg of whiskey on my shoulder. The journey was a long one, thirty-two miles, with a burden and it being summer time was no small undertaking. I arrived however, in East Macon the following day. I entered the woods in search of a clay root where I could hide away my burden. I found a large tree that was blown down, leaving a big hole, where I placed my keg and covered it with leaves. I marked the place so as to find it when wanted. I also carried a canteen full of liquor under my coat, and walked towards Macon. On the way I met a Federal in deep study. I passed him a step or two, then stopped and said, Say! He turned, saying, you speak to me? I said, Yes, would you like to have a drink? He said, Yes, the best in the world. I tell you how you can get this canteen full. If you bring me out a mule this side the sentinel I will give you this canteen full. He remarked, You'll wait yonder until I return. I waited over an hour, when I saw him come on a small mule. The exchange was quickly effected, and I rode back to Milledgeville and left the mule at Stroters. After eating a hearty meal I returned on foot to Macon, I repeated the same tactics, brought back three mules and sold over one hundred drinks at $1.00 a drink, paid Stroter my debt and returned to Washington County, left my stock with my friend B. S. Jordan to tend his crop, who at that time had a negro plowing an old steer. I said, Ben, Work your crop, for I do not know how long you can keep them. I returned to Sandersville in quest of the boys who claimed the captured Confederate wagon, and to purchase it. They agreed if I would bring each a wool hat from Savannah on my return I could have the wagon, which I agreed to. Major Irwin gave me an old set of gears and I was ready to carry freight from Sandersville and Washington County to Savannah for a living, for let it be known that Sherman in his vandalism tore up the Central railroad all the way from Macon to Savannah, Ga., and for eight months after the surrender I continued wagoning hauling freight back and forth, taking the weather as it came, rain or shine, cold or warm.

CHAPTER XXXIII.

My first journey as wagoner to Savannah was a successful one. There was still some cotton through the country that escaped the Sherman depredators. Mr. W. G. Brown let me have two bales. Mr. Pinkus Happ let me have one. My tariff was $5.00 per 100 pounds, and the same returning. I took the Davisboro road from Sandersville, having only two mules hitched to the wagon. I had sent word to Mr. Jordan to meet me with my horse and mule still in his possession. The road was heavy for it was a rainy season and to make it lighter pulling I concluded to have a four mule team. So we put the harness on the horse and mule and hitched them in the lead. About that time a negro I knew, named Perry, came up and made himself useful. I said, Perry, what are you doing? Nothing, Marse Ike. How would you like to wagon for me at $15.00 a month and rations? Very well, said he. Well, jump in the saddle, I am on my way to Savannah. It was about four o'clock p. m. Perry took hold of the line and cracked his whip, when the horse, whose other qualities, except a saddle horse I did not know, commenced to kick in a spirited manner, so as to skin his legs with

the trace chains in which he became entangled, I
had to unhitch him. Mr. John Salter was present and saw the whole proceeding. I remarked,
Well. I am sorry for that for I had expected to
have a four horse team, and now can have only
a spike team. Salter said, Hermann, what will
you take for this horse? You say he is a good
saddle horse? I never straddled a better one.
What will you give me? He said he had no
money but had two bales of cotton under his gin
house and I could have it for the horse. How
far do you live from here? Two miles only.
All right, the horse is yours. Perry, let us go and
get the cotton. Mr. Salter led the way where
the cotton was. We loaded the same and drove
that night to the Fleming place and camped.
The trip was uneventful. We made the journey
to Savannah in four days. There was a firm of
cotton factors named Bothwell and Whitehead
doing business in the City, and they were my objective point. However, before arriving into
the city, about thirty miles this side, I met men
wanting to buy my cotton. They offered me
from fifteen to fifty cents per pound. I did not
know what the value was; I knew that before the
war started it brought about eight cents. However, I drove up to the firms office on Bay street.
I saw Mr. Bothwell; after the usual greeting I

said, What is cotton selling at? It brought .62½ this a. m., but I think I can get more than that if it is good cotton. To make matters short I got .65 per pound and the two bales Salter let me have for my horse weighed 600 pounds a bale, netting me $720.00. I bought me another mule and now I was again fully equipped and made the voyage regularly every week. I took a partner, as the business was more than I could attend to by myself; his name was Solomon Witz. He would engage freight during my absence, and we sometimes made the trip together. The country was forever in a state of excitement. New edicts appeared from time to time from Washington, D. C., Congress promulgated laws to suit their motives, and notwithstanding the agreement between General Lee and General Grant at Appomattox that the men should return, build up their waste places and not again to take up arms until properly exchanged and they should not be molested as long as they should attend to their daily avocations, Congress established what was then known as the Freedmen's Bureau, seemingly for the protection of the negroes, as if they needed any, as their devotion to their master and their behavior at home while every white man able to bear arms was at the front fighting for their homes

and firesides, leaving their families in the hands
of their slaves whose devotion was exemplary,
was not that a sufficient guarantee of the relationship between slaves and masters? The attachment was of the tenderest kind and a white
man would have freely offered his life for the
protection of his servants; but that condition did
not suit our adversaries. Although we thought
the war was over, it was not over and more terrible things awaited the Southern people. Emissaries of every description, like vultures, surnamed carpetbaggers, for all they possessed
could be enclosed into a hand bag, overran this
country to fatten on the remnants left. School
mams of the far East, of very questionable reputation, opened what were called schools, presumably to teach the negroes how to read and
write, but rather to inculcate into their minds
all sorts of deviltry, embittering their feelings
against their former owners and life long
friends, urging them to migrate for unless they
did they would still be considered as bondsmen
and bondswomen, thus breaking up the kind relation existing between the white man and the
negro. And all this under the protection of the
Freedmen's Bureau backed up by a garrison of
Federals stationed in every town and city
throughout the Southern States. In fact the

South was made to feel the heels of the despots. Military Governors were appointed. All those who bore arms or aided or abetted in the cause of the South were disfranchised, the negro was enfranchised and allowed the ballot, with a military despot at the helm and negroes and carpet baggers, and a few renegades such as can be found in any country, as legislators. The ship of state soon run into shallow waters and was pounded to pieces on the reeves of bankruptcy. Taxes were such that property owners could not meet them and they had the misfortune to see their lifelong earnings sacrificed under so called legal process, of the hammer, for a mere song. These were the actual conditions in the days of the so called reconstruction. Bottom rail on top, was the slogan of those savage hordes.. Forty acres and a mule, and to every freedman, Government rations, was the prelude of legislation. Men who took up arms in defense of their sacred rights could not be expected to endure such a state of affairs forever, the women and children must be protected. The garrisons were gradually withdrawn; the carpet baggers remained and ruled; negroes formed themselves into clubs and organizations under their leadership, when as an avalanche all over the Southern states appeared the K. K.

K.'s, called the Ku Klux Klan, or the Boys Who Had Died at Manassas, who have come back to regulate matters. Terror struck into the ranks of the guilty and of the would be organizers and the country soon resumed its normal state, Governors fled and Legislators took to the bush. But I am deviating from my subject.

CHAPTER XXXIV.

On the following trip to Savannah I met G. W. Kelley and Dr. G. L. Mason, on the same errand, viz. hauling cotton to market. After having disposed of the same we reloaded our teams in merchandise, which was easily disposed of, as the country was in need of everything that could add to the comfort or even necessities of the people. The country being in the condition it was, we were glad to travel together for company's sake. So in the evening we left and camped about twelve miles out of the city. As a rule one of the party ought to have been on guard, but such was not the case that night. About midnight I awoke and found two of my mules gone. I noted also that the line with which they were attached had been cut with a sharp knife. Following the tracks they led back into the city. So I left my partner at Savannah on the lookout while I went my way back to Sandersville, minus two mules. I managed to buy two more mules to fill out my team. I had to take what was offered to me, at any price, my partner, after remaining several days at Savannah, recognized one of the mules in charge of a negro. He called for the police and had the negro arrested. There being no legal judge, the case was carried before a captain of one of the military companies stationed there. The negro proved by a confederate that this mule was in his possession long before my partner claimed it was stolen, thus setting up an alibi, without proving as to where he got her from. My partner failed to get the mule and had to pay about $8.00 costs for his trouble, which was all the cash he had with him. Later the firm received a bill for $5.00 more cost but I paid no attention to it and never heard of it any more.

Under the advice of their instructors, the blacks were going and coming. The road to Savannah was traveled by them at night as well as by day. Most of them were making for the cities. Savannah was the goal for those in this section. One evening on my way I stopped my team within eighteen miles this side of the City. Mr. Guerry, who was a fairly well to do farmer for those days and conditions, near to whose domicile I camped, buying some corn and fodder from him to feed my team, also such provisions for myself as he had for sale. At break of day we had left on our weary journey; on my return a day or so afterwards I passed his premises and to keep from walking I had bought me an extra mule. As I rode up I noticed Mr. Guerry and three of his sons in a pen, ready to kill hogs. It was on a Friday, in the month of December, 1865. It was a clear, beautiful, cold day. I greeted them, Good morning, gentlemen, this is a beautiful day to kill hogs. Without noticing my greeting, one of them said, "This is the fellow," when the old fellow picked up his gun from the fence corner and raising the same exclaimed, "You are the d——d fellow that took off our cook." I was completely taken by surprise, and the first word I spoke I said, "You lie", and I jumped off my mule and drew my pistol. My neighbors say they saw her follow your wagon the day after you camped here the night before. I said, In fact we caught up with a negro woman about two miles from here carrying a large bundle on her head, and she asked my driver if she could put her incumbrance on the wagon. I said, No, my mules have all they can pull, and are jaded already. In fact that was all the words that passed between her and me and up to about 10 o'clock a. m. she was either walking in front or behind the team, carrying her luggage. I did not know where she came from nor where she was going. I supposed she was on her way to Savannah, like the rest of them. I guess you see them pass here daily. He said, some of my neighbors told me they saw her behind your wagon. Just at that moment Messrs. L. D. Newsome and Seaborn Newsome. and Alex Brown drove up, hauling cotton to Savannah. I was glad to see them. Hello boys, you of Washington County come in good time. Here are some fellows accusing me of stealing their negro cook. They said at once, Oh, no! You got hold of the wrong fellow. We know him, he comes from our county and would not do such a thing. He is a Confederate soldier and fought all through the war. Then I said, Mr. Guerry, let us reason together. You have always treated me clever when I passed here. I have never entered your yard. I always paid you for what you sold to me. The negroes are free and they are thought to migrate. I had no rights to stop the woman on her journey, but had I known that she was your servant I would have talked to her and advised her to go back where she belongs. Mr. Guerry seemed to regret his hasty words and begged my pardon, and insisted on all of us, to go into the house for refreshments. We finally shook hands and parted good friends.

CHAPTER XXXV.

A rainy season soon set in; the streams were overflowing, and the road became bad and hard, to travel. On arriving at the Ogeechee river at Summertown I found that it had deborted its banks and was at least a quarter of a mile wide. I struck camp, waiting for the water to recede. The following day Geo. W. Kelley drove in sight. He also had a load of five bales of cotton and he struck camp. But it continued to rain and the river instead of receding became wider and deeper. The cotton market was declining rapidly and we were anxious to reach the market. I suggested to Mr. Kelley that I would take the tallest of the mules and sound the width of the current. The mule walked in the water up to the banks, neck deep, when he began to swim, I guided him when again he struck foothold. I rode to the end of the water, in parts only breast deep. I retraced my steps and reported my investigation. We held counsel together and concluded that by using prolongs we could hitch the eight mules to one wagon and while the rear mules would be in mid stream the front ones would be on terra firma and pull the team across. We sent to Mr. Coleman who lived close by, for ropes. We cut saplings, laid them on top of each wagon fastened the ends tight to the wagon body so as to prevent the current from washing off any of the cotton while the wagon would be submerged in midstream during the crossing. Our plan proved to be a successful one, and thus we forded the Ogeechee river without the least accident. We repeated the same tactics for the remaining wagon. We reached Savannah in due time, sold the cotton and bought merchandise for other parties, and I received pay going and coming. On returning I concluded to cross the river by the upper route, at Jenkins Ferry, to avoid recrossing the river as per previous method. We struck camp at dark close to the river bank. I told Perry to feed and water the team while I would examine the ferry flat. Presently Mr. Stetson from Milledgeville, drove up and also struck camp. I considered the flat a very shabby and a dangerous affair to cross on with a heavy load and so reported, but Mr. Stetson thought it all right. The following morning at break of day the ferryman was on hand as per arrangements that evening. Stetson and his men hurried up so as to get across first and thus gain time. My man Perry also hurried faster than was his wont to do, for he was usually slow in his movements, when I cautioned him to take his time and go slow and let the other wagon cross first. It was well that I did so, for the flat went down nearly midstream, and if the front mules had not had foot hold in time the whole business would have drowned. Stetson's damage in merchandise was considerable. He was loaded with salt, cutlery and general merchandise. When I saw that no personal damage was done I bid them good bye to take another route by a twenty mile detour, via. Louisville, and crossed the river at Fenn's Bridge.

CHAPTER XXXVI.

The Central road was being rebuilt from Savannah and we met the trains at its terminals, thus shortening the distance of our journeys. The train had reached Guyton, thirty miles this side of Savannah and was advancing daily until completed to Macon. It was early in the spring when I met the train at station No. 6, a flat country. It had rained nearly daily for a week; the roads were slushy, I had on a heavy load; we had traveled the whole day long until dark. It was hard to find a dry knob to camp on, until finally we came to a little elevation. I said Perry we are going to stop here. He guided the team into the woods a few paces and unhitched, while I was looking for a few lightwood knots to build up a fire. Everything was wet and it was hard to kindle up a blaze. When suddenly there arrived on the scene an ambulance pulled by a team of four splendid mules and thirteen Federal soldiers alighted. They took the grounds on the opposite side of the road. I thought to myself, Now I am into it. Perry was on his knees, fanning up the damp pine straw, when one of those fellows called, Heigho, you black fellow, come here. I said to Perry in an undertone, Attend to your business. When the same fellow called again, Hello you negro, I told you to come here, did you hear me?' accompanying his remarks with the coarsest words. Perry answered, My boss told me to tend to my business. D——n you and your boss, too, was his reply. As he had completed the sentence, I being close by the side of my wagon, reached up and took my Spencer in hand, bringing it from a trail to a support. I stepped to the center of the road, saying, D——n you some too. This is not the first time I have met some of you at odds, and I am ready for the fray, if it has to be. Everything was quiet, not a word was uttered. I still remained standing in the road, watching any move they might make, when one of them spoke, saying, Will you let me come to you? He spoke in a very conciliatory tone. I said, Yes, one at a time. He came to me unarmed, and said, Let us have no trouble; don't pay any attention to that fellow, he is drinking. There is plenty of room here for all of us, without any friction. I said, Well, if your friend is drunk, take care of him. I am able to take care of myself. He returned to his camp and I to mine. I heard him say to his comrades, That fellow won't do to fool with. By that time Perry had succeeded in having a rousing fire and we went to work on the culinary department. Our meals were simple, a little fried meat and corn bread and water from out of a ditch. Presently one of the Federals hollered over, "Say, Johnnie, don't you want some coffee?" I answered, "No, it has been so long since I tasted any I have forgotten how it tastes." He said, We have a plenty and you are welcome to it if you will have it. I said I have no way to make coffee if I had any. So one of them came over with some parched coffee and offered it to me. I declined it, for I had no mill to grind it, nor any vessel to stew it in. They insisted, bringing over all of the paraphernelia for the brewing of coffee and I must admit that it was enjoyed by Perry, as well as myself, it being the first that had pssed my lips in four years. After our meal was completed they came over, one after another and sat around the fire. The conversation became general and I found them to be very congenial company. One brought me a whole haversack full of green coffee, saying, Have it, we have a sack of over a hundred pounds. I thanked them saying, This is quite a treat. And what seemed to be a disagreeable affair in its incipiency terminated most agreeably. It having become late I suggested that we take a night cap and retire. I passed around the jug and each returned to his respective quarters. However I slept, as the saying is, with one eye open. Early in the morning we fed the mules, rekindled the fire, drank a warm cup of coffee and ate a bite or so. We harnessed two of our mules, two of which in the lead were of small size, when one of the Federals proposed to swap mules. I said, Your mules are worth a great deal more than mine, and I have no money to pay boot. We don't want any money said another, we want you to have the best team on the road, by swapping your two lead mules for those tall black ones of ours you will have a real fine team. They then said they were on their way to Augusta to report to the quartermaster there, that they had receipted for four mules and a sack of coffee to be delivered to the quartermaster in Augusta. The mules in their possession were not branded as government mules but were picked up and a mule is a mule, so we deliver the number of heads is all that is required. To tell the truth I feared a trap, but while I was talking with one of them the others changed the lead mules for two of theirs and off they drove in a lope, singing, Old John Brown Lies Buried in the Ground, etc. We trudged along, Perry and I elated over our good luck, when Perry said, Well Marse Ike, your standing up to them made them your friends.

CHAPTER XXXVII.

I had rented the store house from Mr. Billy Smith where he and Slade had done business before the war, in Sandersville, and opened up business in heavy and family groceries. In the meantime my team was making the trip between Sandersville and the Central terminal, which had not considerably advanced, owing to the demoralized condition of labor. So I concluded at this particular time it would accelerate matters by hauling a load of merchandise with my team; hence I drove through all the way to Savannah. While there, on passing Congress street, I met an old friend named Abe Einstein, of the firm of Einstein and Erkman, wholesale drygoods merchants. He was speaking to one Mr. Cohen from New York, who had just arrived by steamer with a cargo of drygoods. He wanted to locate in Augusta, but owing to the Federals having torn up that branch of the railroad at Millen the Augusta trains run no further than Waynesboro. Hence he was trying to fill in the gap with teams. Mr. Einstein told him that I had a splendid team and that I would be a good man for him to employ. So he asked me if I would haul a load for him. I replied I would if he would pay me enough for it. He said, How much can you pull at a load? I said, My mules can pull all that the wagon can hold up. What do you ask? Four hundred dollars. Whiz, I did not want to buy your team, I only wanted to hire it. I said to him, Well, that is my price. I said, You fellows up North tore up the road, you ought to be able to pay for such accommodations as you can get. He studied over the situation a little. Turning to Mr. Einstein, Do you know this man; can I rely on him? Mr. Einstein replied, Perfectly reliable, I stand sponsor. He said, I tell you what I'll do, I'll pay you down $200.00 and Mr. Einstein will pay you $200.00 when you return. Mr. Einstein agreed to it, so I said, That is satisfactory, I shall deliver so many boxes as you put on to the agent, take his receipt for the same and Mr. Einstein will pay me $200.00 due. I had, to my regret, had to discharge my teamster Perry, owing to the neglect of duty, and engaged another named Bill Flagg. He was an old conscientious negro, very religiously inclined. We loaded our team and followed instructions. On arrival at Waynesboro, I never had been there before, so I inquired for the depot and found an improvised little house beside the railroad track and a man claiming to be the railroad agent. I have a load of goods here for Augusta. Put them in the car said he. I said, count the boxes and make me out a receipt. He said all right. After my business with the agent was concluded, I asked him to show me the Louisville route, which he pointed out to me, with several explanations as to the right and left intervening roads. Waynesboro was at that time, as it is now, the county site of Burke county, a town of about 1000 inhabitants. It has greatly improved since and is quite a prosperous city of some importance now.

Before we got out of the incorporation a detachment of Federal troops surrounded my team and ordered my driver to dismount. I was a few paces behind my wagon and I hurried to the front. One of the soldiers had hold of my mules' bridle and ordered my driver to dismount. I said to my man, If you dismount I will kill you; you sit where you are, you are under my orders. I ordered the trooper to let go my mule. He turned loose the bridle, but held his position with others in front of the team. The commotion brought together the balance of the garrison and some citizens. I remarked right here, I'll sell out; you shall not deprive me of the means to make an honest living. So the Captain remarked, We are ordered to take up all Confederate property. I said, I have no objection for you to take up Confederate property, but this is my individual property and your action is highway robbery, which I do not propose to submit to. There is a way to prove those things; I am a citizen of Sandersville and have been wagoning for a living. There is a garrison of troops in my town and if this is Confederate property they have had a chance to confiscate it long ago. He said, What is your name? I answered, I. Hermann, Sandersville, Washington County, is my home. He pretended to make a note of it and told me to drive on. I was glad to have gotten out of that scrape. On reaching home Flagg came to me, saying, Boss, I have to quit you. What is the matter, Bill? said I, have I not always treated you right. Oh yes, but I am afraid of you. How so Bill? I am afraid some day you might get mad with me and kill me: Any man that can stand before a whole company of Yankees like you and keep them from taking his team, is a dangerous man. You must get you another man. I said, all right, Bill. When Perry heard that Bill Flagg had left my employment he came to me, asking to be re-instated and promising to be more attentive to his duties. So I took him back and he remained with me for several years.

CHAPTER XXXVIII.

The railroad track had advanced considerably, and in the Fall of the year, 1866, had reached Bartow, No. 11. My partner for some time had taken charge of the team while I attended to the store. Once he came home badly bunged up and a knife cut on his cheek. I said, What has happened? He said he had some difficulty with the Agent and they double teamed on him. So I remarked, Well, you can send Perry without you going. I wrote to the agent asking him to deliver to the bearer, Perry, a load of my merchandise then in his possession, to check off the same and send me a list. We had at that time two car loads on the track for the firm. When Perry returned he failed to bring the list, his wagon being loaded with corn and every sack ripped more or less. I said, How come you to accept merchandise in that condition. He answered, the sacks were allright when I took them out of the car, it was after they were loaded one of them fellows, a white man named Smith, run around the wagon and cut the sacks and I spilled lots of corn. I picked up some of it and put in that sack, indicating a sack ¾ full. I said, Do you know the man; would you recognize him again if you were to meet him? Oh yes, Marse Ike. Saturday morning I took charge of the team and my partner remained at the store. I took dinner and fed my mules at my friends' Mr. B. G. Smith, to whom I stated the facts as told to me. He said, be careful, don't be too hasty. I said, Right is right and I dont want anything but my rights, and those I am going to have before I return.

We arrived at our destination about four o'clock p. m. The Sherman contingency had burned the warehouse as they did all the others along their march. Consequently the railroad Company used passenger cars on the side track to transact their office work, while freight cars served as a warehouse until discharged of their contents. As I entered the office car a young man met me. I remarked, Are you the agent? He said, No, Mr. Mims is at Parson Johnson's house. What is your name? My name is Smith. Then you are the scoundrel that mutilated my goods, and I advanced. He run out of the door and slammed it to with such force that he shattered the glass panel into fragments. When I came out to where Perry was, he said, That's the fellow that cut the sacks, there he goes. Well Perry build a little fire by the side of this car for here we will camp until some one returns to deliver us the freight. The sun had set below the horizon and it had begun to get night, when Mr. Tom Wells, an acquaintance of mine, approached me. He was an employee of the railroad company also. Well Ike, old fellow, how are you getting along? All right Tom, how are you? I am all right. What brought you here, said he? I said business, I have goods here if I can find an agent to deliver them. I heard you came here for a difficulty, said he. I remarked, It seems I am already in a difficulty, I can't get any one to deliver me my goods. Well, I will tell you, Mr. Mims is a perfect gentleman. I am glad to hear it. Do you know him? No, I have never seen him, but up to now I can't have the same opinion of him that you have. I have not been treated right and I came here for justice. He said, Well, let me tell you; there are about forty employees here, hands and all, and they will all stick to him, wright or wrong. I said, I came here to see Mr. Mims and I intend to stay here until I do see him, if it takes me a week. Well Ike, if you promise me that you will not raise a difficulty I will go after him and introduce you to each other. I said, Tom, there are other ways to settle a difficulty without fighting if men want to do right. Well I will go for him; I know Mr. Mims is going to do what is right, and you too. Mr. Mims came presently, and a whole gang following him. I said, Mr. Mims, it seems you and my partner had a difficulty. I do not know the cause and I do not care to know. He said you fellows double teamed on him and he got worsted in the fight. To avoid a recurrence of the difficulty I sent my driver to you and a note. You ignored my note and sent me a load of corn with all the sacks ripped open, more or less, with a knife in the hands of one of your employees. I berated my man for accepting goods in that condition and he stated to me how all of it was done. I am now here to see what can be done about it. I have never done you any injury to be treated in that manner. He said, Mr. Hermann, I am sorry it happened. I will see that it will not be done again. I said, Have you discharged the fellow who did it? He answered, No, not yet. I said, Well, I demand that it be done now. And what about the damage I sustained. He remarked that the road would run to Tennille by next Wednesday, a distance of 25 miles, and he would forward my two car loads of freight free of charge from Bartow to Tennille. I said that was satisfactory. I wanted to load my wagon; he said, we do not deliver goods at night. I answered that if he had been at his post of duty on my arrival I would have had plenty of time to load and be on my way back, and I wished to load up at once for the morrow being Sunday I did not want to be on the road. He delivered the merchandise and Perry and I passed Sunday with my friend B. G. Smith, who was glad matters passed off as they did. Monday morning we took an early start and by twelve o'clock I was at home. That was my last trip as a wagoner, but not as a soldier, as the sequel will show.

CHAPTER XXXIX.

When the commanding officers of the Confederate army surrendered and stacked arms the rank and file expected that the terms of the cartel promulgated and agreed upon would be carried out to the letter. The men laid down their arms in good faith, feeling as General R. E. Lee remarked in his farewell address to them, that under present unequal condition it would only be a waste of precious lives to continue the struggle. The following were the terms of the agreement entered into between General Grant and General Lee: The officers and men to return to their homes and remain there until exchanged and not to be disturbed by the United States authorities so long as they observe their paroles and the laws in force in their respective states.

But the fellows who directed the ship of state and who were invisible on the firing line became invincible, when the South lay prostrated. The first order was from Secretary Staunton, for the arrest of our commanding officers. This order, however, was resented by General Grant as contrary to the cartel and should not be executed. This caused a rupture between the two and the order was finally rescinded. The next step was to disperse all State authority and appoint a military Governor. General Wilson acted in that capacity in Georgia. The same year, 1865, negroes were proclaimed free and military garrisons established in every town, city or village throughout the South. Under the superintendence of those militaries the Freedmen's Bureau was established, forcing negroes to migrate from one place to another, thus breaking up the good relationship still existing between Masters and servants. The bureau was seemingly gotten up for the protection of the blacks, as if they needed any protection, they to whom we owed so much for their good behavior during the time when every available man able to bear arms was at the front, leaving their families in charge of the negroes. The gratitude of our people was or ought to have been sufficient guarantee in that line. Such harmonious condition did not suit the powers that be, there was venom in their heart for revenge, and punitive measures were concocted. Never were captives bound tighter than the people of the South. Is it a wonder that the men of the South became desperate and used desperate remedies to oust more desperate diseases? The carpet baggers made their exit. The negroes' mind had been prejudiced under the auspices of those vultures. They were forced into societies, one of which was the Rising Sun. Some called it The Rising Sons. God only knows what ultimate result they expected to obtain. Drums and fifes were heard in every direction at night times. The woods were full of rumors that the negroes are rising. Men in towns made ready for emergencies, every one on his own hook; no organization for defense, in case harsher measures should be needed. When the author of this sketch took up the idea of a reunion of his comrades and inserted a call in the county's weekly, calling on the members of Howell's Battery for a social reunion, their wives and children, when other veterans suggested why not make it a reunion for all the veterans of the County. I was only too glad for the suggestion and changed the call to include all veterans of the county, and on the day specified there was the greatest reunion Washington County ever had. It was estimated that eight thousand people participated. There were over one hundred carcasses besides thousands of baskets filled to overflow with eatables and delicacies. The object of the meeting was stated to form an artillery company as a nucleus or rallying head and to meet organization with organization not as a measure of aggression but as a protection. The author was elected Captain. Under his supervision he built an armory and eventually the State furnished him with two pieces of artillery. The day he received the guns he had a salute fired. The boys in the rural districts had not forgotten the sound of artillery and the town was filled with enthusiasm. Some of the negro leaders called on me to know what all that means, I told them it was to teach their misguided people that we can play at the same game and if they don't stop beating their drums and blowing fifes in the night time when honest people are at rest I would shell the woods. This admonition had a splendid effect and the people of Washington have lived in peace ever since. The author resigned his commission in the year 1881, when Honorable Alex Stephens was Governor of Georgia. And Washington County has the honor of having inaugurated the first reunion of Confederate veterans. The citizens of Washington County and Howell's Battery presented the author with a gold headed ebony cane, beautifully carved, as a memorial and their regard for him as a citizen as a soldier. Being taken by surprise I had to submit to the caning.

War Between the States 261

The South passed seemingly through the chamber of horrors of the Spanish Inquisition and punishments administered by degrees. First robbing the owners of their slaves, of their justly acquired property, after they, (the North), received from the Southern farmer its full equivalent in U. S. money. Second, in the promulgation of the Civil Rights Bill, in April, 1866. Third, in forcing the Southern people to accept the 14th and 15th amendment to the Federal Constitution, not as a war measure, as Abraham Lincoln claimed, when issuing his proclamation to free the negroes, but as political measures to perpetuate themselves in power.

Georgia, Alabama, Arkansas, Louisiana, South Carolina and North Carolina refused to accept those conditions and in consequence were not admitted into the Union until 1868, although paying enormous taxes without representation, and finally had to submit in self defence. Virginia, Texas and Mississippi held out until 1870 before they succumbed to the thumb screw.

CHAPTER XXXX.

In writing the foregoing reminiscences I came near omitting an incident that unless inserted would make them incomplete. In 1868 I went to New York, via. Charlotte, North Carolina. It was a long journey by rail, on account of many disconnections and lay overs. On arriving at Greenville the South Carolina Legislators had adjourned in Columbia and boarded the train enroute for Washington, D. C. to see General Grant inaugurated as President of the U. S. The body at that time was composed of a mongrel set of coal black negroes, mulattoes and carpet baggers. Cartoosa, a mulatto, was then Treasurer of the State. A negro named Miller was General in chief of the S. C. militia of State troops. They came prepared to have a regular holiday. They carried large willow baskets full of the best provisions and champagne by the quantity, all at the expense of the State of South Carolina. On arriving at Aqua Creek, which was about 5 o'clock p. m., we took the boat up the Potomac and were furnished with dinner. When the bell rang, one of the South Carolina Legislators, a coal black negro, took his seat at the table when one of the waiters, also a negro, whispered in his ear. He replied in a very boisterous manner that his money was as good as any white man's. The waiter reported to the Purser, who took the would be gentleman by putting two fingers in his collar, lifted him up and gave him a kick that sent him reeling into the engine room. The white carpet baggers seemed not to have noticed this little side show. However the black brute continued his boisterous remarks and abusing the white race, and that he, a South Carolina representative had his dignity grossly insulted and that he was going to report the incident to General Grant on arrival. When an old gentleman who must have been between 65 and 70 years of age could not stand his abuse any longer, although the balance of the passengers were amused at his discomfiture took a pistol from his coat side pocket, shoved it near the negro's face and remarked, I stood that abuse as long as I intend to; one more word and I'll send you to hell where you belong, you black brute. The representative, seeing that this man meant what he said, kept mum. The South Carolina delegation undoubtedly made a report at headquarters of the above incident, for in the winding up of President Grant's inaugural address he expressed the following sentiments: That he hoped that white and black races would conform to the situation and that by mutual good conduct would maintain the peace and harmony so necessary for both races, or words to that effect.

Arriving in New York I took in the City. It was my first trip there since I had landed at Castle Garden from the four masted schooner, The Geneese, nearly ten years previous. I visited the large firm and emporium of H. B. Claflin & Company and spoke to Mr. Bancroft. I gave him a statement of my commercial standing, such as it was, and asked for his advice, as it was my first attempt as a dry goods merchant. My means being very limited I wanted to make them reach as far as possible. He treated me very courteously and furnished me with a salesman, whom he introduced as Mr. McClucklan. On our way to the basement he asked me, What State? I said Georgia. D——n Georgia. I stopped at once, looking him squarely in the face I said, You can't sell me any goods, I am going for some one not prejudiced against my State, and started back, when he exclaimed, Hold on, you misconstrue me; I have been a prisoner at Andersonville and I hate the name of Georgia. I do not mean to say that there are no good people in Georgia, like everywhere else. Noting a keystone that I wore on my watch chain he said, I see you are a Mason? So am I, displaying a square and compass pinned on the lapel of his coat. We can talk together said he. If it had not been for a brother Mason I don't think I'd be here today, I think I would have died of starvation. He told me of his transit from Andersonville to the Coast. When the train stopped at a country station, the name of which he did not know but he knew it was on the Central railroad, he gave the words of distress. It was a dark night, he could hardly have expected anybody to answer it, but someone did and before the train left some one brought him enough fried ham and biscuit to last him several days. So I said, It was wrapped in a home made napkin with blue borders. He looked at me with astonishment, saying, So it was; what do you know about it. I said, I am the fellow, and told him what I did and that Mrs. Hardwick commended me for it and would not take any pay and that the station was Davisboro. The man was beside himself. He hugged me, tears ran down his cheeks; he acted like a crazy fellow. He said, You can't buy any goods today, you are my guest. He ran to Mr. Bancroft to get excused, saying that I was an old friend and that he wanted to get off that day. He hired an open carriage and we drove over the whole city, showing me everything worth seeing. He carried me around to a fine restaurant and ordered an elaborate dinner, spent his money with the most lavish hand, regardless of my protestations, for he would not let me spend a copper. The following day I made my purchases. It is useless to say that he dealt squarely with me and with his advice and experience I made what small capital I had purchase me a very decent stock of merchandise.

CHAPTER XXXXI.

Again when President Lincoln in 1863 issued his edict to the Commanding Generals in their respective territory to proclaim all the negroes free, as a war measure, as he claimed, he attempted on a large scale what John Brown failed to make a success of on a small scale, namely to create a servile insurrection, and thus exposing the helpless and defenceless to the rapacity of semi-savage hordes. But it failed, as all other attempts in that line have failed, thus again proving the good relationship existing between the masters and their servants. Compare the situation now with that of the anti-bellum days. When a white emissary from the North hired a horse and buggy from the proprietor of the hotel in Sandersville, Washington County, Georgia, and left with the same for parts unknown, he was finally located in Florida and captured and brought back and put in jail. The lock of the jail was so rusted for the want of use that it took the assistance of a locksmith to open the door to let him in. How is it now? A commodious building has had to be erected to accommodate the masses who trample under foot the laws of their country; the jails and chaingangs are full to overflowing, with the perpetrators of crimes. Those are the results of the so called reconstructionists. Lynching was an unknown quantity in those days; there was no necessity for it. The laws of the country were administered, justly and loyally. Courts met at regular periods and often adjourned the same day for the want of patronage. Some say we are progressing. That is true, but in the wrong direction. Retrogressing is the proper word to apply, especially in morality.

CHAPTER XXXXII.

Another illustration worthy of mention in connection with the others is related here. A friend of mine named John J. Jordan, wounded at Vicksburg, Miss., one of the cleverest and inoffensive beings, owned several slaves by heritage. Among them was one John Foster, a mulatto. He was an accomplished carpenter and very active. His master gave him his own time and he was comparatively free all his life, he was devoted to the Jordan family and was a very responsible negro, however, his newly made friends the carpet baggers filled his brains with such illusions that he became a leader among the negroes, making speeches and made himself very obnoxious to those who were his friends from infancy. All at once Foster disappeared. He was gone a couple of years when his former master received a letter from him, dated New York, begging assistance to enable him to return to Washington County. Notwithstanding his master's impoverished condition, the money was sent him and Foster came back entirely reformed. He had no more use for the Yankees, his short stay among them cured him. What a pity the authoress of Uncle Tom's Cabin did not take John Foster under her protecting wings. What a lost opportunity! What a fine additional illustration that picture would have made to her already fertile imagination as the sequel will show.

One day John Foster came to my house to see me. Good day, Marse Ike, said he, I thought I'll come to see you it has been a long time since I sawn you, and the following conversation took place: Where have you been John? I've been to New York. How do you like New York? I don't like it at all, let me tell you Mass Ike, those Yankees are no friends of the negroes. Well John I could have told you so before you went. Mass Ike, let me tell you what they've done. They told me I could make a fortune in the North, that I could get four and five dollars a day by my trade as a carpenter. Who told you so? Why John E. Bryant and his like of carpet baggers. Well did you not get it? I got it in the neck, I tell you what they did. I left here with right smart money, Marse John let me pay him for my time and got nearly three hundred dollars that I saved. I went to New York, and after looking around the city for a few days I commenced hunting work, but whereever I went they shook their heads, for no. I

War Between the States 271

spent the whole winter there without striking a lick until I spent all my money. I finally applied at a shop where a dutchman was foreman, I was willing to work at any price for I had to live but do you know what they did? No John, I don't. Well they every one of them, and they worked twenty-five hands, laid down their tools and walked out of the shop declaring that they would not work by the side of any damned negro, and the boss had to discharge me. No, Marse Ike, the Yankees are no friends to we colored people, only for what they can cheat us out of. I worked all my life among white folks here at home and it made no difference, I tell you Marse Ike, the people of the South are the negroes friends. Well John, you did not say so before you left here. No, I did not appreciate what the people here done for me until I went North. Well, John, you ought to go among your people and disabuse their minds and tell them what you know from personal experience. I am doing that Marse Ike every day. I have not long to stay here below, I have contracted consumption from exposure and am hardly able to do a day's work. I am taking little jobs now and then. Well John, if you stand in need of anything come to see me. You will always find something to eat here and some clothes to wear. John died six months later.

CHAPTER XXXXIII.

Before concluding these reminiscences I take pleasure however in stating that Capt. Howell and myself met after the surrender and after a thorough understanding agreed that honors were easy and by mutual consent to bury the hatchet and eventually became warm friends. A little incident, however, is worth relating here. I was a delegate to a Governatorial Convention from Washington County. Capt. Howell also was a delegate from Fulton County, the vote was very close. We were each for the opposing candidate, the convention lasted for several days and could not agree. Capt. Howell came to see me, stating that he was a committee of one appointed by the caucus to come to see me and influence me to change my vote and vote for their candidate. I said "Capt. what did you tell them"? He said, "I said I doubt very much that my influence would have any effect, darn him I could not do anything with him when I had the power to control him and I am satisfied that my mission will be in vain." I said, "you spoke well, Captain, go back and report failure.

Conclusion.

I would be derelict in my duty and the gratitude I feel towards the noble women of the South who shared the brunt of misery while their loved ones were at the front suffering the hardship and rigors of camp life, and were fighting the battles for what they deemed their most sacred duty. With aching heart and burning tears she bade her dear ones God speed and a safe return, shouldering all the responsibilities of providing for those who were left behind and not able to provide for themselves. Did they stop at that? Many delicacies and garments were sent to the front by them to cheer those in the field. They organized wayside homes for those soldiers who were in transit. They visited the hospitals and administered to the sick and wounded. They organized the ladies relief association and in every way imaginable added to the comfort of those who shared the brunt of battle. The Confederate veterans felt grateful to their wives, daughters and kinswomen who banded themselves together under the name of U. D. C. They have proclaimed in songs and stories the righteousness of the Confederate cause and even at late date forced our adversaries to admit that the cause we fought for was

"I've stood that abuse as long as I intend to; one more word and I'll send you to hell, where you belong—you black brute."

right and the Courts so hold it. Would it be too much to ask the United Confederate Veterans to see that enduring monuments of imperishable material be erected in the capital of every Southern State to perpetuate the memory and the fidelity of those noble heroines?

Sparta heroism was tame indeed in comparison with that of Southern women, especially those who were left in the wake of the invading armies amidst the ruins of a once happy home. It is a half a century that has elapsed since the thunder of Fort Sumter shook this hemisphere. New generations have appeared on the scene, fraternization is progressing slowly, but surely, the past is relegated gradually to the rear and the States again assert their rights, as they see it. Therefore it behooves the National administration to see to it that equal rights to all and special privileges to none, is its duty to enforce so as to maintain this nation the greatest nation on the globe. The sections must get together and look to the wants and needs of their associates and as far as lies in their power assist in bringing relief. Thus past differences will vanish and brotherly love will again prevail and this United States of America will forever be united to stand in bold relief the model government in the world.

APPENDIX A.

List of Officers of the Washington Rifles.

Capt., S. A. H. Jones.
1st Lt., J. W. Rudisill.
2nd Lt., B. D. Evans.
3rd Lt., W. W. Carter.
Ensign, C. M. Jones.
1st Sergt., E. P. Howell.
2nd Sergt., G. W. Warthen.
3rd Sergt., J. M. G. Medlock.
4th Sergt., A. D. Jernigan.
5th Sergt., P. R. Taliaferro.
1st Corpl., W. J. Gray.
2nd Corpl., A. T. Sessions.
3rd Corpl., W. H. Renfroe.
4th Corpl., John R. Wicker.
Color Bearer, J. T. Youngblood.
Surgeon, B. F. Rudisill.

List of Privates.

Allen, G. R.	Arnaw, James
Bailey, J. W.	Boatright, B. S.
Barnes, A. S.	Barnes, M. A.
Barwick, W. B.	Brantley, J. E.

Brown, Jos. M.
Curry, David
Curry, J. S.
Cullen, S. E.
Cullen,, E. W.
Clay, W. S.
Cason, W.
Dudley, J. A. Q.
Durden, M.
Fulford, T. B.
Flucker, M. R.
Grimes, W. B.
Gilmore, T. J.
Gilmore, E.
Gaskin, J.
Haines, C. E.
Hines, W. H.
Hines, S.
Hicklin, A. F.
Hermann, I.
Jordan, N. J.
Jordan, J. J.
Jones, S. B.
King, Jas. R.
Knight, W. G.
Knight, W. K.
Layton, J. H.
Lewis, W. H.
McCroon, J. J.
Morgan, John H.
Matthews, W. C.
McDonal, J. J.

Collier, Ed.
Curry, S. K.
Curry, J. H.
Cullen, W. A.
Commings, G. E.
Cason, G.
Cook, A. T.
Dudley, W. H.
Fulghum, J. H.
Fulford, S.
Gray, W. B.
Gilmore, J. N.
Gilmore, S. M.
Godown, James
Haines, S. S.
Haynes, T. H.
Hines, A. C.
Hines, R.
Hicklin, W. P.
Honard, W.
Jordan, J. T.
Jones, W. H.
Kinman, W. H.
Kitrell, G.
Kelley, G. W.
Lamb, I.
Lawson, W. H.
Lewis, W. B.
Medlock, E.
Mason, G. L.
Massey, S. N.
McDonald, A.

Newsome, J. J.
Orr, T. A.
Parnell, R. J.
Roberts, J. B.
Roberson, W. G.
Robison, R. T.
Rodgers, L.
Rawlings, C.
Renfroe, J.
Scarboro, A. M.
Smith, J. C.
Smith, J. H.
Smith, John H.
Solomon, H.
Spillars, J.
Trawick, A. J.
Tyson, T. L.
Tarbutton, G. A.
Veal, R. H.
Whiddon, B.
Warthen, T. J. W.
Wall, W. A.
Wagoner, W. H.
Wicker, T. O.

Newsome, J. K.
Peacock, G. W.
Pittman, W. H.
Parker, W. J.
Roberson, J. A.
Robison, W. R.
Riddle, A. M.
Rawlings, W. H.
Stanley, J. S.
Stubbs, J. N.
Smith, J. P.
Smith, W. H.
Slate, S. L.
Sheppard, J. J.
Tarver, F. R.
Trawick, J. T.
Tookes, C. C.
Turner, N. H.
Whitaker, G. W. II.
Whiddon, M. M.
Wall, C. A.
Waitzfelder, E.
Wessolonsky, A.
Watkins, W. E.

APPENDIX B.

The Newnan Guards, A.—Capt. Geo. M. Harvey.

The Columbus Guards, B.—Capt. F. G. Wilkins.

The Southern Rights Guards, C.—Capt. J. A. Hauser.

The Oglethorpe Light Infantry, D.—Capt. J. O. Clark.

The Washington Rifles, E.—Capt. S. A. H. Jones.

The Gate City Guards, F.—Capt. W. F. Ezzard.

The Bainbridge Independents, G.—Capt. J. W. Evans.

The Dahlonega Vols., H.—Capt. Alfred Harris.

The Walker Light Infantry, I.—Capt. S. H. Crump.

The Quitman Guards, J.—Capt. Jas. S. Pinkard.

J. N. Ramsey of Columbus, Ga., was elected Colonel.

APPENDIX C.

1st. Lt. John W. Rudisill became Capt. of Compy. C. 12 Ga. Battalion.

2nd. Lt. Beverly D. Evans became Col. 2nd. Ga. State troops.

3rd. Lt. W. W. Carter became Capt. Compy. G. 49 Ga. regiment.

Ensign C. M. Jones became Capt. Compy. H. 49 Ga. Regiment.

1st. Sergt. E. P. Howell became Capt. of Martins Battery.

4th. Sergt. A. D. Jernigan became Capt. Compy. H. 49 Ga. Regiment.

5th. Sergt. P. R. Taliaferro became Capt. Compy. E. 32nd. Ga. Regiment.

1st. Corporal W. J. Gray became 1st. Lieut. Sandersville Artillery.

2nd. Corp. A. T. Sessions became Lieut. Compy. B. 12 Ga. Batalion.

3rd. Corp. W. H. Renfroe became Lieut.

4th. Corp. J. R. Wicker became Lt. 32 Ga.

Private G. R. Allen became Lt. 57 Ga.

Private James Arnau became Lt. 49th Georgia.

Private B. S. Boatright became Lt. 12th Georgia Bat.

Private James M. Brown became Lt. 5th Georgia Reserve.

Private M. R. Flucker became Orderly Sergt. 12th Georgia.

Private T. J. Gilmore became Lieut. Martins Battery.

Private Wesley Howard became Corp. Martins Battery.

Private J. T. Jordan became Col. 49th Georgia Regiment.

Private W. H. Jones became Lt. 32nd Georgia Regiment.

Private S. B. Jones became Capt. 8th Georgia Cavalry.

Private James R. Kinman became Lieut. Company B. 12th Georgia Bat.

Private W. G. Knight became Sergt. Company B. 12th Georgia Bat.

Private Isaac Lamb became Lt. 53rd Georgia.

Private W. H. Lawson became Capt. 5th Georgia Reserve.

Private W. C. Matthews became Capt. 38th Georgia Regiment.

Private J. J. Newsome became Capt. Company E. 12th Georgia Bat.

Private Geo. W. Peacock became Lt. 12th Georgia Bat.

Private J. B. Roberts became Capt. Company D. 49th Ga. Regiment.

Private W. J. Parker became Capt. Cobbs Legiose.

Private W. G. Robson became Lt. Martins Battery.

Private J. A. Robson became Sergt. Company B. 12th Ga. Bat.

Private H. T. Robson became Sergt. 12th Georgia Bat.

Private J. N. Stubbs became Sergt. 12th Georgia Bat.

Private J. C. Smith became Lt. 12th Georgia Bat.

Private H. Soloman became Capt. 14th Georgia Regiment.

Private G. A. Tarbutton became Capt. Hillards Legion.

Private G. W. H. Whitaker became Capt. 12th Ga. Batt.

Private Benj. Whiddon became Capt. 5th Georgia Reserve.

Private T. O. Wicker became Adgt. 28th Georgia Regiment.

Private W. E. Watkins became Sergt. Company B. 12th Georgia Bat.

APPENDIX D.

Robert Martin, known as Bob Martin, from Barnwell, S. C., was elected Captain.

Evan P. Howell, 1st Lt.
W. G. Robson, 2nd Lt.
Reuben A. Bland, 3rd Lt.
H. K. Newsome, 1st Sergt.
S. J. Fulform, 2nd Sergt.
W. H. Hines, 3rd Sergt.
J. B. Warthen, 4th Sergt.
W. H. Dudley, 5th Sergt.
W. M. Cox, 6th Sergt.
Haywood Ainsworth, 7th Sergt.
W. B. Hall, 1st Corp.
W. B. O'Quinn, 2nd Corp.
W. F. Webster, 3rd Corp.
J. E. Cullin, 4th Corp.

Privates.

H. Allen
J. F. Bailey
J. F. Brooks
W. A. Brown
B. L. Bynum

A. C. Hines
J. D. Hardy
Gabe Kittrell
J. E. Johnson
A. R. Lord

W. T. C. Barnwell
M. B. Cox
R. W. Cullen
J. Curry
R. Dixon
R. E. Caudell
W. E. Doolittle
J. E. Ellis
Geo. T. Franklin
E. T. Ford
S. M. Gilmore
J. A. Godown
W. N. Harmon
Gabrill S. Hooks
V. A. Horton
C. Howell
J. J. Hadden
Ben Jones
R. E. Jackson
T. M. Lord
J. E. Mullen
H. C. Lord
J. W. Massey
J. J. O'Quinn
S. B. Pool
N. Raifield
Wm. F. Sheppard
W. L. Stephens
G. W. Thomas
W. H. Toulson
F. A. McCary
J. C. Waller

D. G. McCoy
F. M. Loden
J. B. Oxford
J. H. Pittman
H. L. Skelley
J. F. Salter
W. A. Smith
J. P. Thomas
R. Tompkins
D. B. Tanner
J. H. Veal
J. J. Waller
T. Webster
Simeon Bland
J. Armstrong
Henry Achord
C. Blizzard
T. J. Brooks
J. J. Braswell
T. M. Barnwell
W. B. Barwick
H. L. Cox
T. C. Cullen
A. Dixon
R. L. Campbell
E. D. Chaplen
J. C. Durham
B. O. Franklin
H. Ford
W. R. Gilmore
T. J. Gilmore
W. A. Grimes

G. W. Webster
Geo. D. Warthen
Lawson Taylor
All Armstrong
W. D. Bodiford
W. J. Brooks
B. S. Braswell
W. J. Bell
J. N. Bentley
S. B. Cox
E. W. Cullen
T. A. Curry
J. H. Coleman
D. F. Chambers
T. C. Doolittle
A. E. Erwin
H. Fields
B. Garner
E. T. Gilmore
R. A. Godown
Isaac Herman
H. J. Hodges
R. H. Hales
A. D. Heath

T. J. Hamilton
W. H. Horton
W. C. Howard
L. W. Hines
Red Jones
J. Jackson
F. A. Lockman
John L. Laymade
N. A. Lord
W. J. Massey
W. Oxford
F. Posey
G. B. Rogers
J. F. Sheppard
J. P. Smith
W. C. Thomas
J. F. Tompkins
H. T. Thompson
W. Waller
T. C. Warthen
J. Wood
T. R. Gibson

www.ingramcontent.com/pod-product-compliance
Lightning Source LLC
Chambersburg PA
CBHW032035150426
43194CB00006B/290